Haiti

Haiti

BY MARTIN HINTZ

Enchantment of the World
Second Series

Children's Press®
A Division of Grolier Publishing

NEW YORK   LONDON   HONG KONG   SYDNEY
DANBURY, CONNECTICUT

For Selavi and the lost children of Haiti

Consultant: Karen De Bres, Associate Professor, Department of Geography, Kansas
State University, Manhattan, Kansas

Please note: All statistics are as up-to-date as possible at time of publication.

Visit Children's Press on the Internet at:
http://publishing.grolier.com

Library of Congress Cataloging-in-Publication Data

Hintz, Martin.
    Haiti / by Martin Hintz.
    p. cm. — (Enchantment of the world. Second series)
    Includes bibliographical references and index.
Summary : Describes the history, geography, history, government, people, and culture
    of the second oldest republic in the Western Hemisphere.
    ISBN 0-516-20603-6
    1. Haiti—Juvenile literature. [1. Haiti.] I. Title. II. Series.
    F1915.2.H56 1998
    972.94—dc21   97-25518
                                              CIP
                                              AC

Acknowledgments

There are numerous individuals who assisted in providing background for this work. Special thanks go to Patricia Schutt-Aine and the staff of the Librairie Au Service de la Culture in Port-au-Prince; Prof. Albert Valdman, director of the Creole Institute at Indiana University; agronomist Florence Sergile of the University of Florida; and authors Herbert Gold, Valerie Takavec, and Chelle Koster Walton. A nod also goes to the Center for Strategic and International Studies in Washington, D.C.; Human Rights Watch; and the National Coalition for Haitian Refugees. Thanks also to Dan Hintz, who researched the sidebars and inserts for this book. The author particularly wishes to express thanks to Sejou, Nicholas, Vivianne, Henri, Sandra, Claude, Guesly, Rosie, Joslin, and all their friends. Their courage and strength remain a beacon for all young people around the world.

Contents

CHAPTER

Haitian children enjoy
the beach

Hello to Haiti

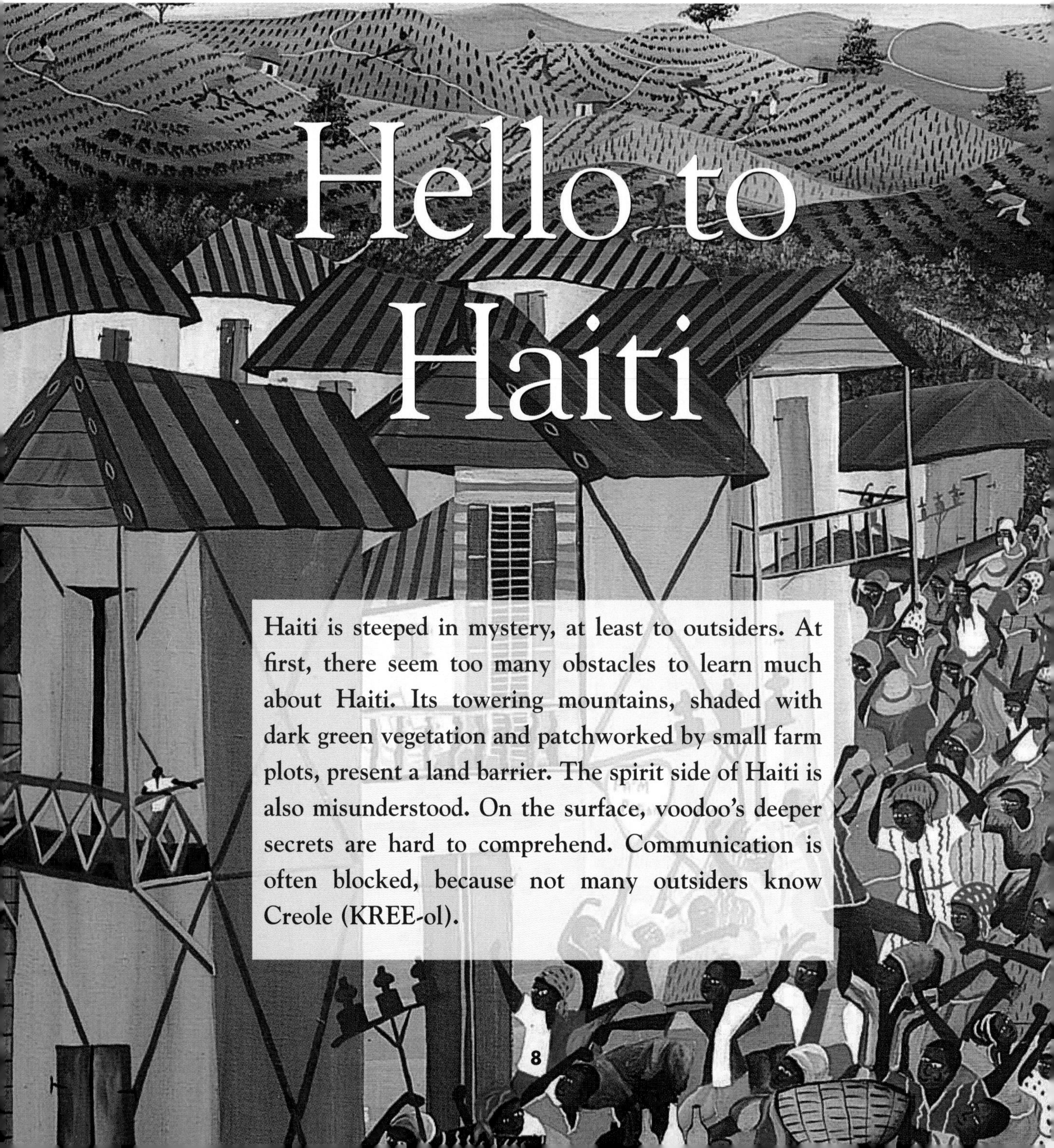

Haiti is steeped in mystery, at least to outsiders. At first, there seem too many obstacles to learn much about Haiti. Its towering mountains, shaded with dark green vegetation and patchworked by small farm plots, present a land barrier. The spirit side of Haiti is also misunderstood. On the surface, voodoo's deeper secrets are hard to comprehend. Communication is often blocked, because not many outsiders know Creole (KREE-ol).

THIS IS ORDINARY HAITIANS' ONE-OF-A-KIND LANGUAGE, which is a melding of French and West African dialects, even though other islands in the Caribbean have their own local languages that are also called Creole. Haiti's official language is French, however, and many Haitians speak English, often learned at school. In addition, the country's often dangerous political world presents another major difficulty in getting things done.

Yet, once outsiders allow themselves to get beyond all this, they discover the delight and wonder of the ordinary Haitian people. Certainly, it will always be hard to reconcile the corruption and violence affecting these hardworking people. Strife and violence, unfortunately, have been part of the nation's heritage since it was founded in 1804. Yet Haitian life is also a mixture of pride, creativity, strength of spirit, and enthusiasm. After all, Haiti is the second oldest republic in the Western Hemisphere, after that of the United States. Haiti always seems to be on a seesaw with this turbulent mix of negatives and positives: up one minute with a democratically elected president, then down with a military takeover; up the next time when Haiti's artists are praised worldwide, then it is down again, because many of the people remain sick and hungry.

Authors Visit

Author Herbert Gold has visited Haiti many times. In one of his books, he called Haiti the "best nightmare on earth." He wrote about the good and bad aspects of life in Haiti, calling the country a nation of unimaginable misery and unpredictable grace.

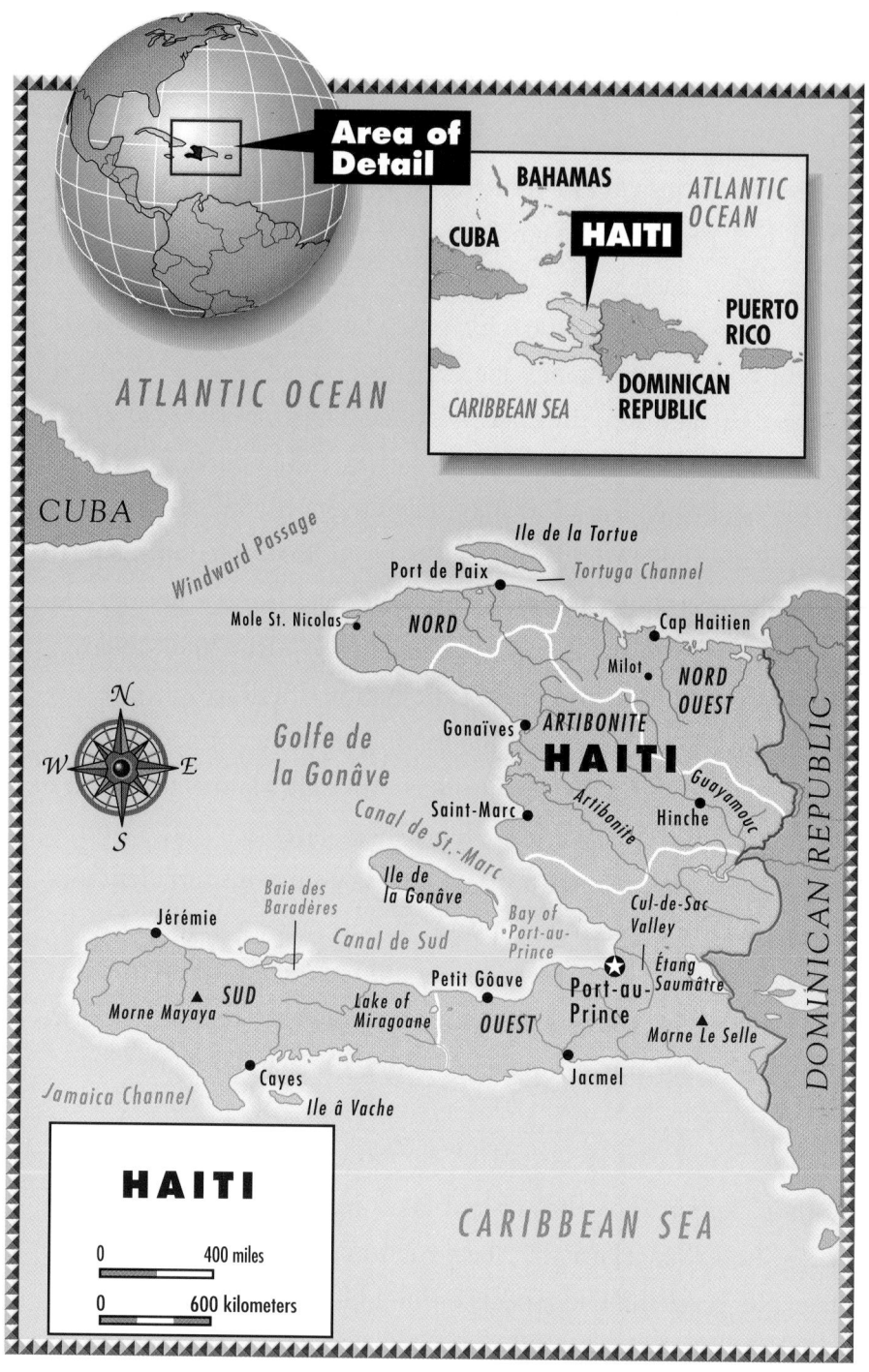

Area of Detail

BAHAMAS
CUBA
HAITI
ATLANTIC OCEAN
PUERTO RICO
CARIBBEAN SEA
DOMINICAN REPUBLIC

ATLANTIC OCEAN

CUBA

Windward Passage

Ile de la Tortue
Port de Paix
Tortuga Channel
Mole St. Nicolas
NORD
Cap Haitien
Milot
NORD OUEST
Gonaïves
ARTIBONITE
HAITI
Golfe de la Gonâve
Guayamouc
Saint-Marc
Artibonite
Hinche
Canal de St.-Marc
Baie des Baradères
Ile de la Gonâve
Cul-de-Sac Valley
Jérémie
Canal de Sud
Bay of Port-au-Prince
Étang Saumâtre
Petit Gôave
Port-au-Prince
SUD
Lake of Miragoane
OUEST
Morne Mayaya
Marne Le Selle
Jamaica Channel
Cayes
Ile â Vache
Jacmel
CARIBBEAN SEA

DOMINICAN REPUBLIC

HAITI

0 — 400 miles

0 — 600 kilometers

Graham Greene, who wrote a novel about Haiti called *The Comedians*, did the same. These two observers took plenty of time to learn about Haiti. They studied the country from the inside and pointed out both the good and the unfortunate aspects of Haitian life. As these authors pointed out, the two go hand in hand.

Many Haitians seeking a better life fled their country by boat.

Over the generations, Haitians fled or emigrated from their homeland to escape poverty, political turmoil, and possible death. Between January 1979 and June 1981, more than 80,000 Haitians entered South Florida seeking a new life. By the 1990s, more Haitian doctors lived in Montreal, Canada, than in all of Haiti. The people had to leave their homeland to find opportunity, hope, and security.

Haitians lined up at a refugee camp in Cuba

In return for the chance to begin a new life, the emigrants brought their spirit and enthusiasm to Canada, the United States, the Bahamas, and the other nations that allowed them to stay. Emigrants include a professor of Africology (African studies) at the University of Wisconsin–Milwaukee. A Haitian Olympic track star now lives in Montreal. A young man born in the small Haitian town of Croix de Bouquet now lives on Long Island, New York, and wants to study law. A Haitian girl was adopted by a family in Indiana and is not sure of her exact age. She wants to work with animals when she grows up. There are thousands more Haitians with other such stories.

Deams of the Future

Now step back to Haiti, tucked on the western third of the island of Hispaniola in the Caribbean Sea. A boy name Henri works on a

Many people work on farms in Haiti.

Fishing is a way of life.

farm with his parents and seven brothers. They live near the town of Port de Paix. He hopes to be an agronomist and study agriculture. Sandra lives in Cap Haitien on the far north coast of Haiti. She dreams of being a nurse. Jean's father is a fisher. He lives on Ile de la Gonâve, a small island in the bay fronting Port-au-Prince. He also wants to be a fisher but would like a larger, more seaworthy boat.

Haitians may live far away from the palm-fringed beaches of their homeland. Or they may remain in Haiti. Regardless, the country's young people have similar dreams and hopes. They want to attend school and have good jobs and maybe a family. Of those who remain, only time will tell if their homeland can give them the stability and economic security they need to achieve their wishes.

The mid-1990s were the first time in generations that

The streets of Port de Paix

Haiti was blessed with even a small bit of peace. Years of dictatorships had taken a toll. Previously, people were scared to speak out against the those who abused them. Many fathers and mothers were out of work. Others barely made enough money to get by. Children were uneducated. The country's economy was a mess. But there was hope for the future with the free election of two presidents. The first, Jean-Bertrand Aristide, needed help from the international community to keep his office. His successor, Rene Préval, was sworn in with no problems. Each promised to help build his country and put it on a firm social footing. They pledged to end violence and keep the peace. They promoted greater freedom and the chance to prosper with extended peace and justice for everyone. Whether all this will come about remains to be seen.

Of course, many problems still remain in Haiti. It takes hard work to change bad habits. Some politicians and business people still want to run the country as if it is their private property. Who knows how the military will respond as the democratic process gains strength. Many of the elite, wealthy Haitians who prospered in the old days need to rethink how they do things. The Haitian constitution is full of words about liberty, concern, and caring. It is now up to everyone in the country to do more than make proclamations. It is now time for positive, caring action.

Haitians demonstrating for democracy

Haiti's Geographic Roller Coaster

It is easy to find Haiti, which occupies the western third of the island of Hispaniola in the Caribbean Sea. Hispaniola is part of a long chain of islands called the Greater Antilles. This is a mass of individual rocks, sandy beaches, and mountains. They rear from the sea in an east-to-west direction south of the tip of Florida. In addition to Hispaniola, other Greater Antilles islands are Cuba, Jamaica, and Puerto Rico. Northwest of Hispaniola, closer to Florida, are the Bahama Islands.

F URTHER TO THE EAST OF HISPANIOLA, IN A WIDE ARC cutting far out into the Atlantic Ocean and then dropping south, are the Lesser Antilles. These are dots of islands with such exotic, sun-kissed names as Martinique, St. Lucia, and Antigua, among others.

Cuba—The Closest Land

The island of Cuba is the nearest land mass to Haiti, being only 50 miles away (80 km) across a body of water called the Windward Passage. The passage is one of the major channels connecting the Caribbean with Atlantic Ocean. Off Haiti's south coast, the Caribbean is relatively shallow. In some places, it is barely 500 feet (152 m) deep. Farther out, the sea bottom is up to several thousand feet deep. Florida, the closest part of the North American mainland, is 750 miles (1,200 km) to the northwest. New York City is 1,365 miles (2,184 km) almost due north of Haiti.

Haiti is part of the island of Hispaniola in the Caribbean Sea.

Geographical Features

Largest City: Port-au-Prince (pop. 752,600)

Highest Elevation: Morne la Selle, 8,793 feet (2,680 m)

Lowest Elevation: Sea level along coast

Total Area: 10,695 square miles (27,700 sq km) excluding offshore islands

Longest River: Artibonite River, 174 miles (280 km.)

Largest Lake: Etang Saumatre, 66 square miles (170 sq km)

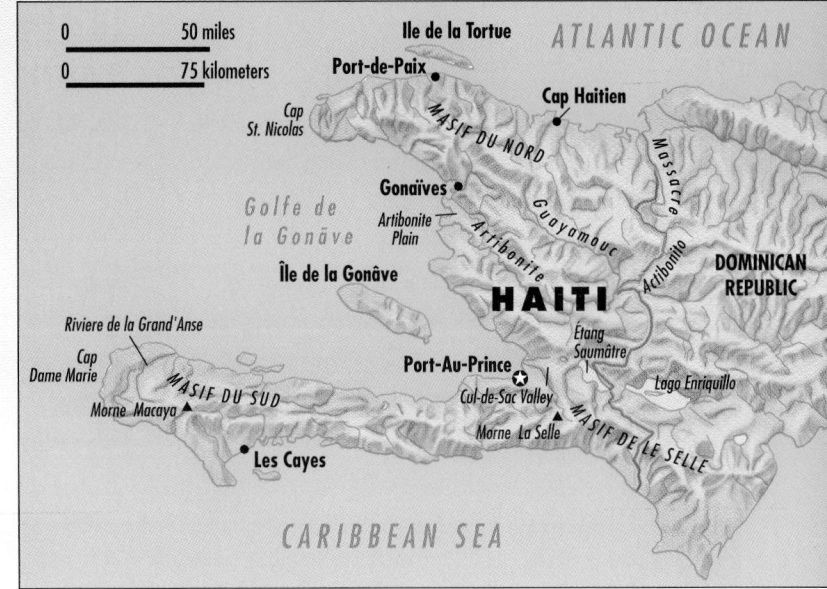

Annual Rainfall: 20 inches (51 cm) in northwest to more than 100 inches (254 cm) on the highlands of the east and south

Average Temperature: 95°F (34°C) in July to 87°F (31°C) in January

Spread out a map and locate the Atlantic Ocean. This vast body of rolling green-blue water washes Hispaniola's rough north coast. The Caribbean Sea's dark green waves creep around the western and southern shores, with their many small beaches. Sailors were always nervous about the underwater reefs that rim Hispaniola's coastline, especially on the Haitian side. Today's visitors only have to fly one hour and forty minutes from Miami, Florida, or three hours from Montreal, Canada, to arrive in the capital of Port-au-Prince. It used

Looking at Haiti's Cities

In the 1700s, Cap Haitien (below) was called the Paris of the Antilles because of its exotic cultural life. The city was founded in 1670 by explorer Bertrand d'Ogeron de la Brouere. Today, Cap Haitien, on Haiti's northern coast, has 68,000 residents. It was destroyed during the Haitian war of independence and was rebuilt by King Henri I. Cruise ships call on the port, with tourists visiting Henri's castle called the Citadelle Laferrière. This fortress is high in the mountains above the city. It was once a four-hour mule trip but now motorcoaches quickly take visitors there. Cap Haitien's average daily temperature in January is a pleasant 87°F (31°C). In June, the temperature is in the mid-90s.

Jacmel is 25 miles (40 km) south-southwest of Port-au-Prince on Haiti's southern coast. It was founded in 1689. The old French city looks like a cross between New Orleans and Paris, with its antique ironwork, balconies overhanging streets, and mellow lifestyle. The city's residents enjoy the many coffeehouses that line the main streets. The community was once the center of Haiti's coffee export business. Several famous Haitian artists still call the city their home. The central marketplace is noted for its crafts, selling everything from goatskin drums to bracelets. The average daily temperature in January is in the upper 80s, with the June temperature hovering around 93°F (34°C).

to take weeks of dangerous sailing from Europe. Now a plane ride from Paris, France, is only ten hours.

A Shared Border

The entire island of Hispaniola covers 29,530 square miles (76,484 sq km) of forests, plains, waterfalls, farmland and high, rugged countryside. This makes it the second largest of the Caribbean islands. Haiti shares a 171-mile (275-km) border with the Dominican Republic, its neighbor on the eastern end of the island. It has a rugged 1,098-mile

Haiti is known for its many mountains.

The Haitian coast has some lovely beaches.

Haiti's Ancient Names

There were three ancient names for Haiti given to the land by its original inhabitants. *Ayiti* was used in the language of the island's residents. There are three root meanings in that word. *A* means flower, *Y* means high, and *Ti* means land or region. Therefore *Ayiti* can be translated "flower of high land," "mountainous land," or "land of high mountains." *Quisqueya*, which means "big land," was the term given to the island by the natives of islands around Haiti. Another name often used was *Bohio*, or "rich in villages."

A view of Port-au-Prince, the country's capital

(1,771-km) coastline with few good beaches. The total area of Haiti is 10,714 square miles (27,750 sq km). This includes the small offshore islands of Ile de la Gonâve, Ile de la Tortue, Grande Caymite, L'île à Vache, and La Grande Caye. Ile de la Gonâve is the largest island, covering 254 square miles (658 sq km) and the tiniest speck is La Grande Caye, at 1.4 square miles (3.5 sq km). There are two long peninsulas at the west end of the country. In between the peninsulas is the Bay of Gonâve. The northern peninsula sticks 100 miles (160 km) into the Atlantic Ocean. The southern peninsula juts 200 miles (320 km) into the Caribbean Sea. From the air, the peninsulas look like giant shark jaws about to devour Ile de la Gonâve, which is swimming in the wide bay.

Although Haiti is small, its rugged landscape and poor roads make travel difficult. The center of the island of Hispaniola is divided into two forested mountain ranges, giving the appearance of a great emerald dot rising from the crisp blue seawater. Great scars of bare, eroded land show up, however. These bare patches show where all the trees have been cut for firewood. Between the two ranges is a low-lying plain extending into the Dominican Republic. This region was once underneath the ocean. But that was in prehistoric days when the earth's crust was being formed millions of years ago.

More than 75 percent of Haiti is made up of these cliffs, valleys, and towering peaks. The Haitians say that "God took Haiti in his hand and crumpled it up." There is even a story about explorer Christopher Columbus, who discovered and named Hispaniola. Upon his return home, Columbus showed the Spanish king and queen what the island looked like. To illustrate his tale, he wadded up a piece of parchment. The resulting bumps on the paper readily showed how rugged landscape was.

Haiti's mountains cover 8,108 square miles (21,000 sq km) of the landscape. There are only 2,606 square miles (6,750 sq km) of flat land. The highest mountain is in the western region of Haiti. This is Morne la Selle, which soars 8,793 feet (2,680 m) into the clear, sun-scoured sky. The next highest peak is Morne Macaya in the southern region at 7,700 feet (2,347 m). You can quickly spot two more high mountains in the west. These are Morne du Cibao, at 7,480 feet high (2,280 m), and Morne Bois-Pin, at 7,333 feet (2,235 m). It is no wonder that the ancient Arawak Indians called this the "mountainous land." The mountains seem high because they are so close to sea level.

Columbus at Hispaniola

The Republic of Haiti itself is a bit smaller than Belgium. That Western European nation covers 11,781 square miles (30,513 sq km). Haiti is about the size of the state of Maryland, which covers 10,577 square miles (27,394 sq km) in the eastern United States.

Few Flat Areas

While few relatively level areas are in Haiti, the broad central plain around the city of Hinche covers 840 square miles (2,170 sq km).

King Henri Christophe's Fortress

The Citadelle Laferrière of King Henri Christophe (above) is a colossal fortress in northern Haiti's mountain region. He started building the towering structure in 1805 to protect the country from possible French invasion. King Henri (statue shown at right) wanted a fort that would hold 5,000 soldiers up to three years in case of siege. It is estimated that 200,000 persons labored on the Citadelle's construction. Work was still in progress when the king died in 1820. The fort, built at an altitude of 2,970 feet (900 m) overlooks the surrounding deep mist-shrouded valleys. It covers 26,400 square feet (8,000 sq m) with its 12-foot (4-m) thick walls. One room was large enough to hold 45,000 cannon balls. The cannon are still lined up outside, as if still waiting to be fired. The building is now on the UNESCO world heritage list of protected sites.

Other flat stretches of ground are scattered here and there, like bits of tablecloth spread out across the jagged landscape. Some patches are as small as 17 to 19 square miles (45 to 50 sq km) in width.

Etang Saumatre is a large salt lake in Haiti, covering 66 square miles (170 sq km) with its brackish, undrinkable water. The lake is located at the extreme eastern end of the Cul-de-Sac Valley near the city of Port-au-Prince. The lake is 13.6 miles (22 km) long and 7.4 miles (12 km) wide.

Two other fresh water bodies in Haiti are the Lake of Miragoane (9.7 square miles or 25 sq km) and Trou Caiman (6.2 square miles or 16 sq km). There are ten rivers and numerous small streams flowing down from the mountains. The two most impressive rivers are the Artibonite and the Riviere de la Grande Anse, with their torrents roaring over the rocks toward the sea. Unfortunately, many of the beautiful waterways are polluted. They carry sewage and are used for washing clothes and for bathing.

Haiti lies in the tropics, where air conditioning is appreciated. Shorts are the uniform of the day for kids. Temperatures are generally constant, ranging from 70°F to 90°F (20°C to 30°C). The hottest time of the year is between March and November, with temperatures peaking in July and August.

People use the waterways for washing clothes and bathing.

The country is shaped like a giant horseshoe, opening toward the west and backed by the mountain ranges. For this reason, the country's interior seldom gets cool breezes, except in the highlands. As a result, Port-au-Prince has one of the highest average temperatures of any major city throughout the Caribbean. Haitians who live in the mountains enjoy the most pleasant temperatures in the hot summer because it gets cooler the higher they climb. Some wealthy Haitians live in an attractive settlement above the capital called Petionville, where they can enjoy the refreshing breezes. The coolest months overall in the country are December, January, and February.

Shorts are common because of the warm climate.

Dry Season

The climate from December through March is quite dry because the towering eastern mountains cut off the trade winds from the sea that bring rain. However, be prepared with an umbrella between May and November. This is the wet time of year, when sudden showers occur regularly. But the rain seldom lasts for more than a couple of hours. Because it usually pours in the evening, everyone expects to get wet if they do not carry an umbrella. But nobody cares if they are soaked. The warm breeze that always comes after a shower is refreshing.

Rainfall amounts vary around the country, depending on the wind and the closeness to the mountains, sea, or plains. Some areas can get up to 100 inches (2,540 mm) a year. A nearby valley tucked into the shoulder of a mountain crest might only have 20 inches (508 mm).

Although the surrounding ocean is generally calm, Haiti is reg-

ularly hit by fierce hurricanes. These storms rage out of the sea most often in late August through September and sometimes on into October. Hurricane winds can reach up to 150 miles (241 km) per hour. They knock down everything in front of them, from buildings to power lines. The resulting high surf can lift up boats and carry them inland, dropping them off in someone's front yard. Haitians heed the storm warnings and head to the safety of the high country to escape the waves and wind.

One of the worst hurricanes in history battered Haiti from October 3 to 8, 1963. Hurricane Flora smashed its way over the island. The storm's fury killed more than 2,500 Haitians, destroyed crops, and demolished homes. Because trees had been cut down for firewood, nothing held back mudslides that swept down the mountains. The towering walls of slippery muck buried terrified people and animals as it swept over roads and buildings.

Haiti was devastated by Hurricane Flora in 1963.

The ruins of Sans-Souci Palace

Earthquakes

Hurricanes are only one kind of natural disaster that affects Haiti. Earthquakes are another. One of the most serious quakes in Haiti's history hit in 1842. It was powerful enough to destroy the sprawling Sans-Souci Palace, the royal residence of King Henri. The palace, in the northern Haitian town of Milot, was designed to rival the magnificent crystal-and-marble Versailles Palace in France. It was

Land on the Move

Earthquakes are common in Haiti because the country's complex landscape rests on sliding plates of rock thousands of feet below the earth's surface. When the plates shift or are jolted for some reason, the earth's crust, or ground surface, rolls or shakes. This is called a tectonic (TEK-tonic) earthquake. This movement regularly happens throughout the island region linked by the Caribbean Sea and Gulf of Mexico. Damage is caused, however, only when the underground movement is powerful enough. There are many small quakes that are barely felt. Earthquakes might start because of a change in the barometric pressure (pressure of the atmosphere as measured by an instrument called a barometer). Or a quake might even be started by some astronomical cause, such as a gravitational pull by the moon swinging closer to the earth. Even seismologists, the scientists who study earthquakes, do not know all the reasons.

168.3 feet (51 m) long and 82.5 feet (25 m) wide, built of hand-crafted brick. But it took only minutes for the building to be shattered and its occupants to be scurrying to safety. Those who did not escape were crushed by the falling walls and ceilings. The palace ruins remain a major tourist attraction. More than half the population of Cap Haitien was killed in that catastrophe.

Haiti, with its mist-shrouded valleys, waterfalls, and high cliffs, is sometimes called the Switzerland of the Caribbean. Switzerland is a mountainous country in Europe. But unlike in Switzerland, it never snows in tropical Haiti. That fact is probably appreciated by the majority of Haitians.

One of the breathtaking waterfalls of Haiti

The Tired Land

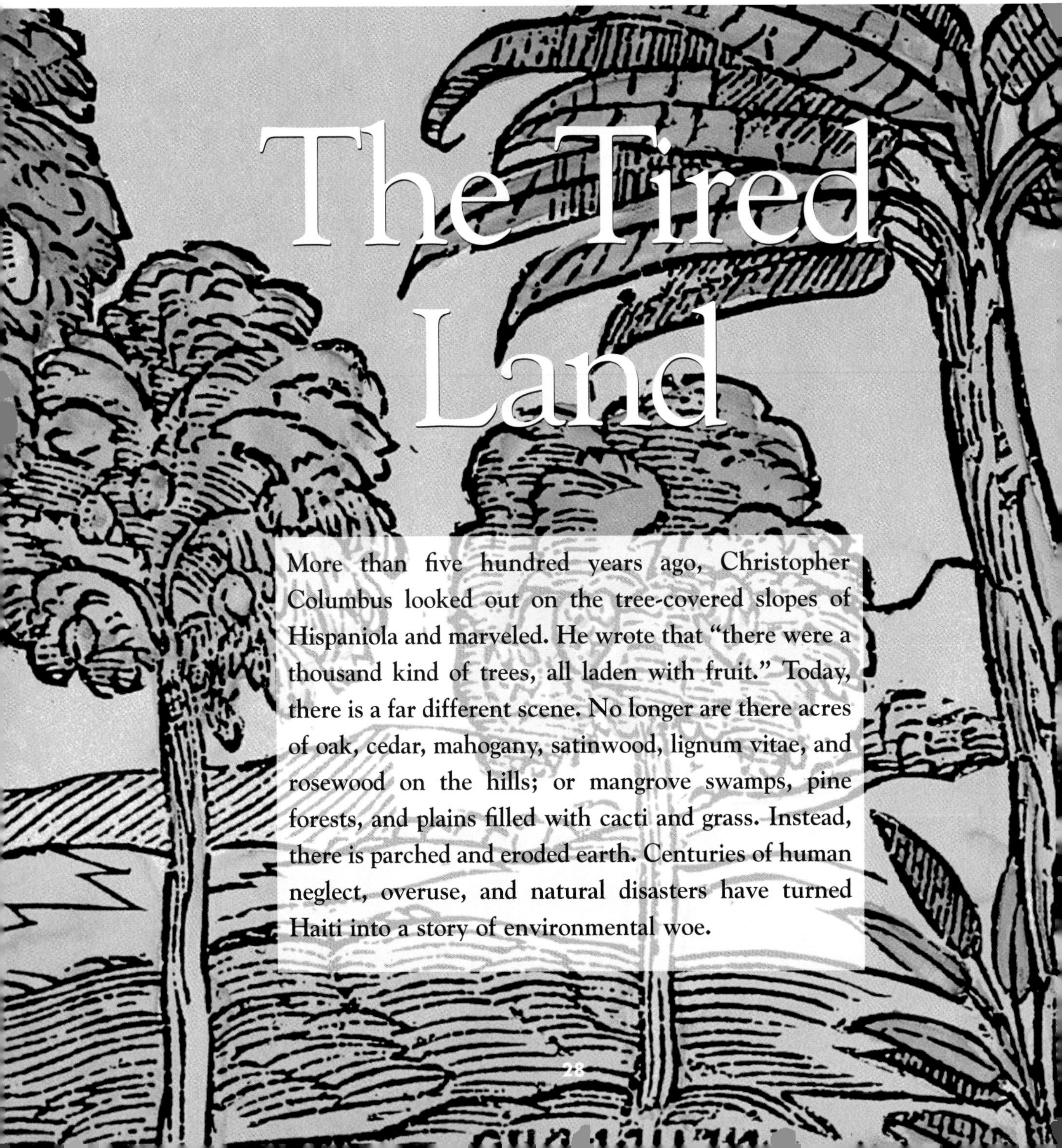

More than five hundred years ago, Christopher Columbus looked out on the tree-covered slopes of Hispaniola and marveled. He wrote that "there were a thousand kind of trees, all laden with fruit." Today, there is a far different scene. No longer are there acres of oak, cedar, mahogany, satinwood, lignum vitae, and rosewood on the hills; or mangrove swamps, pine forests, and plains filled with cacti and grass. Instead, there is parched and eroded earth. Centuries of human neglect, overuse, and natural disasters have turned Haiti into a story of environmental woe.

THERE ARE THIRTY-FIVE PROTECTED AREAS SCATTERED around Haiti. They range in size from 10 to 6,000 acres (4 to 2,428 ha), each being a mosaic of the country's remaining plant communities. The Macaya Biosphere Reserve is the largest of these special plant and animal communities. The reserve is located on a mountain in southwestern Haiti, midway between the cities of Cayes and Jeremie. The native pine forest sweetly scents the air with its resin. The tree branches whisper as they sway in the cool mountain air.

Within the preserve are 102 species of fern, 141 types of orchids, 99 kinds of moss, and many other sorts of rare vegetation. Among its animals are eleven species of butterflies and nineteen types of bats.

Haiti's Animals

The Parc La Visite, about five hours from the resort community of Kenscoff above Port-au-Prince, is another important animal and plant preserve. Scurrying amid the trees are two rare endangered mammals. One is the tiny nez longue, or solenodon, an animal that looks like a shrew with its brown fur, long snout, and tail. Because it eats insects, it is called an insecti-

Parc La Visite

The solenodon eats insects and snails.

The hutia is about the size of a cat.

vore. It also eats snails. In its constant quest for food, the solenodon rustles about the base of the towering pine trees on Mount Macaya.

The other endangered animal living in the park is the hutia. This is an Arawak Indian name. The cat-sized hutia is a rodent like the porcupine, but it has golden-brown fur. It gnaws on the bark of trees. The hutia and its relatives used to be plentiful throughout the Greater Antilles. Few hutia remain. Since Indian and early Spanish days, the little animal has been a food delicacy. The Macaya reserve is the only haven remaining in Haiti where both the solenodon and the hutia are now safe.

There are seventy-three species of brightly feathered birds in Haiti. One of the most beautiful is the white-winged warbler. This bird is very secretive, hiding wherever there is dense tropical vegetation. Another is the chat tanager, a bird that Haitians say looks like a flying pickle because of its greenish coloring. Then there is the Hispaniolan white-winged crossbill with its odd-looking overlapping beak. The black-capped petrie is often seen near the ocean. This high-flying seabird is the size of a crow, easily spotted with its ring of dark head feathers. It nests only in Haiti's steep cliffsides.

The Hispaniolan parrot is another of Haiti's birds. This bright green chatterbox is hard to spot amid the tree leaves. But its *ca-caw-ca* shouting is loud and distinctive. The parrot is becoming more rare. People like the bird as pets. This is a mistake, however, because the parrot seldom survives the sticky lowland heat. Then there is the tiny Hispaniolan emerald. This hummingbird is very friendly and not frightened by humans. The male has a long, forked tail and velvety black patch on its throat.

Parrots are one of the many endangered species of Haiti

Bay Fort-Liberte is another protected site on Haiti's north coast. A special coral reef lies just offshore. The coral are tiny living animals. But when they die, their hard skeletons cement together after centuries underwater. They form vast underwater ridges that make protective homes for hundreds of varieties of sea creatures. Grouper, sea bass, sharks, octopi, eels, and many other species drift, swim, crawl, and float through the reefs. The site is like an underwater freeway alive with holiday traffic because so many marine animals can be found here.

Beyond a small, narrow sandy beach fronting the bay are thousands of towering cacti, some more than 10 to 16 feet high (3 to 5 m). This is one of the largest concentrations of cacti in the Caribbean.

Ecological Disaster?

Other than these few protected areas, much of Haiti's once lush, green landscape has been changed, perhaps forever. Some scientists say the country is teetering on the edge of an ecological disaster because of deforestation, the result of the widespread cutting of trees. Now, wide sections of Haiti may be permanently damaged. Up to 40 percent of the land has been stripped of all its vegetation and more acres are being taken every year. In 1986, it was estimated that 30 million trees were cut down. Ten years later, the number dropped to about 20 million trees because there were fewer to harvest. What

Haiti's National Bird: Hispaniolan Trogon

There is no national animal for Haiti, but the Hispaniolan trogon is Haiti's national bird. The reason for this choice is obvious whenever the trogon is seen swooping through Haiti's forest tangle.

Its blue-and-red feathering reflect the country's national colors. The trogon has feathery red underpants, a blue-and-white tail, a honey-yellow beak, and a gray chest. It was selected as national bird in a vote by schoolchildren taking part in an environmental education program.

will happen in another ten years is almost too scary to consider, scientists agree.

But there are warnings about what might happen if this situation continues. In 1976, the village of Fre Charles was surrounded by a wooded marsh. Today, it is a sunbaked desert. All the nearby trees were cut down for making charcoal that was then sold in the cities for fuel. The people had to go farther and farther away to find wood. Soon, all the saleable wood was far beyond reach. The local residents starved or moved away because nothing else grew on the desolate land.

The Haitian landscape has been hurt by overuse.

There are many reasons for this problem of deforestation. Much blame rests on the shoulders of previous governments that did not care about the nation's ecology. The various dictatorships were concerned only about making money to enrich the elite power structure. They did not devote any government funding to help Haitian farmers find better means of production. When the cash crops failed in one area, the farmers chopped down trees in another region. They needed open land for growing food. They could also sell the wood. The government made only feeble attempts to change these destructive habits.

Unloading sacks of charcoal

But other reasons made it hard to coordinate a conservation campaign. The history of Haiti lay the groundwork for the difficulties. Colonists stripped away the forest cover for sugar plantations. They used so much of the wood to operate sugar mills that within a generation they needed to import lumber for construction. The 1791 slave rebellion also left a scorched and scarred landscape. Through ten years of warfare, few crops could be grown. Armies on both sides burned fields and orchards so their enemies would not get any food.

Transporting the crop from a sugar plantation

After Haiti gained its freedom, most of the world ignored the country. But even as the plantations were destroyed, one element of French law survived the revolt. This rule allowed property to be divided up among the sons when the father died. This caused a disaster for Haiti. Over several generations, the land was divided so much that once large properties eventually became barely an acre or two. This means that almost every inch of land is needed to grow food to support a single family. As Haiti's population continues to grow, the peasants ask, "Why should the trees live, when my children die?"

Haiti's Farmland

Most of Haiti is mountainous. The best farmland is in the central valley along the slow-moving Artibonite River. There is barely enough arable, or productive, land to share. Too many people try

Lore of the Trees

Despite the deforestation of the countryside, there has always been a deep love and respect for trees in Haiti. African tradition has kept this belief alive. In fact, the voodoo spirits, the loa, are thought to live in trees, especially the silkcotton or mapou. Therefore, many groves are considered sacred by the people.

With another folk tradition, a newborn baby's umbilical cord is buried and a fruit tree is planted over the site. The tree and its fruit then belong to that person for the rest of his or her life.

**A voodoo ceremony under
a sacred mapou tree (above)**

**Some voodoo spirits are
thought to live in the
silkcotton tree (right).**

farming on the little land on the steep hill-sides and in the deep valleys. Some Haitians have plots high in the mountains. They tie a rope around their waists and secure them-selves to a rock or tree to avoid sliding downhill when they cultivate their ground. Usually, the farmers are not interested in crops that take a long time, such as trees. Because most rural Haitians are always on the edge of starvation, they need food—and fast. Their farming practices are not good for the worr

have time ... rvesting. ...side the decent ...n small protect ...ot all. envi- from trou- ther

too dry and too wet. Drought dried up the good earth, allowing the wind to blow it away. Heavy rains then caused floods. To make the situation worse, several hurricanes crashed into Haiti.

Yet, almost in spite of what people have done to Haiti's land, there are some areas that continue to be relatively productive.

Workers tilling rice

An irrigation canal

Water and Power in Port-au-Prince

There have been attempts to irrigate the Artibonite Valley to better regulate the water flow. The huge Peligre Dam was almost completed in the late 1950s, when dictator François Duvalier took power. But, his corrupt, violent government drove away the foreign aid that helped start the dam's construction. The structure was never properly completed and could not control the water the way it was supposed to. The dam was also intended to generate electricity. But by 1990, it was in such disrepair that Port-au-Prince only received four hours of electricity a day. No one is sure when it will be fixed and able to provide the necessary hydroelectric power that Haiti needs.

Lake Peligre was created by the Peligre Dam on the Artibonite River.

Sugarcane grows well on the central plains. And yams, onions, congo peas, beans, potatoes, and fruit trees in the area above Port-au-Prince. Rice can be grown in watery, low-lying areas.

Sisal, a plant used to make twine, is also a cash crop. The cassava, a tropical plant with starchy, edible roots, is a staple food. Cassava is pounded into a fine paste for making bread dough.

Where the land is left alone, it brings forth beautiful blossoms. Vibrantly colored orchids, bougainvillea, and fuchsia seem to find life in every crack in the rock.

Sisal drying in the sun

Reforestation

International organizations are not blind to Haiti's problems. Many agencies attempt to help. In the late 1980s, the United States Agency for International Development (USAID) started a reforestation program. Aid workers handed out free tree seedlings to peasants. More than 22 million trees were then planted throughout Haiti. As many as 40,000 farmers participated in the project.

The program is still proceeding slowly. Of course, the farmers need to see results and are disappointed if the trees die or do not seem to grow fast enough. Only about half those planted actually survive. Therefore, many of the special trees that are now being planted are extremely hardy. They grow quickly in almost any type of ground. One of the best is the leucaena. When this tree is cut down, the stump remains and quickly sprouts again. This ensures a new crop of wood about every four years.

Environmental Program

The University of Florida has an agronomy and environmental education program called Haiti-Net. It is staffed by native Haitians such as Florence Sergile. She earned her bachelor's degree in agronomy from the Faculty d'Agronomie in Port-au-Prince and a master's degree at the University of Florida. The project has an office in the Haitian capital with exhibits on the environment and a library on natural resources. Schoolchildren tour the center to

A lush grove of poinsettias and bananas

learn what they can do to help their country recover from its problems.

For a time, even teachers were able to study environmental problems. They wanted to learn about conservation and the environment. This program ended in 1992, however, when the military deposed President Jean-Bertrand Aristide. After the president's return in 1994, the projects were not restarted because of the lack of money.

Even by the late 1990s, there was no other real action on the part of the Haitian government to solve the deforestation problem and the soil depletion.

A river suffering from soil erosion

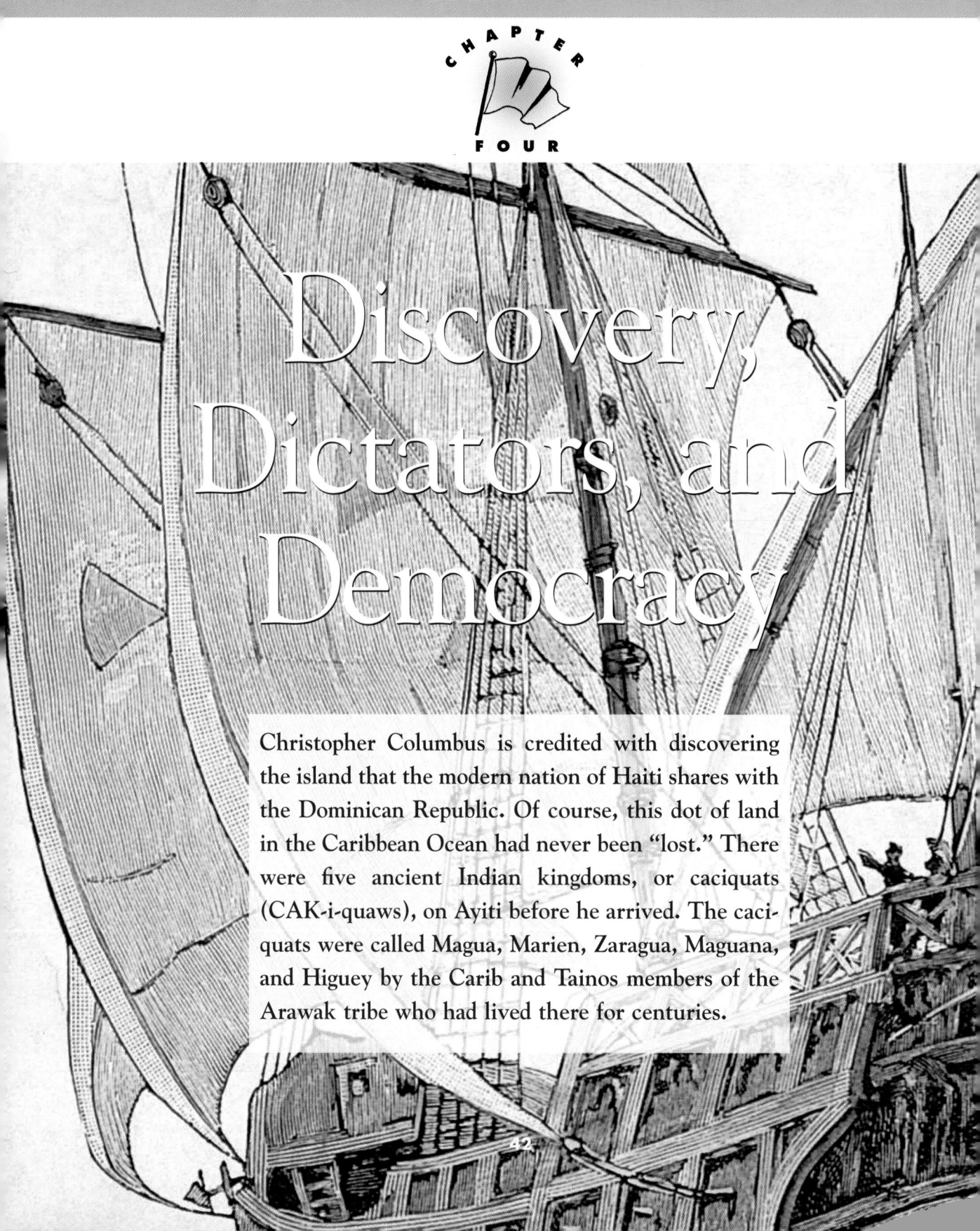

CHAPTER FOUR

Discovery, Dictators, and Democracy

Christopher Columbus is credited with discovering the island that the modern nation of Haiti shares with the Dominican Republic. Of course, this dot of land in the Caribbean Ocean had never been "lost." There were five ancient Indian kingdoms, or caciquats (CAK-i-quaws), on Ayiti before he arrived. The caciquats were called Magua, Marien, Zaragua, Maguana, and Higuey by the Carib and Tainos members of the Arawak tribe who had lived there for centuries.

BUT, OF COURSE, COLUMBUS WAS NOT aware of that when his ships anchored off a spit of land he called Mole St-Nicolas on the northwestern end of the island in 1492. Columbus had left Spain earlier that August. He was seeking a safe, quick trade route to China where he knew were treasures of gold and silk. He thought by sailing west from Europe he would eventually land in the Orient. But instead, he discovered a whole new world, unknown to Europeans.

After crossing the uncharted Atlantic Ocean, Columbus had made landfall in the Bahamas by October. That chain of low, sandy islands lay just to the north of Hispaniola. Columbus then spent several weeks poking around the clear waters of the region.

Columbus Arrives

It was a clear day on December 6, 1492, when Columbus arrived on the Hispaniola coast. One of his ships, the *Santa Maria*, was damaged on the offshore reefs on Christmas Eve. The ship ran aground near what is today the city of Caracol in northeast Haiti. Columbus

The term Hispaniola is mostly now internationally used for the island that is occupied by the mostly Creole-speaking Republic of Haiti on the west and the Spanish-speaking Dominican Republic on the east. Creole is a mixture of French and West African dialects dating back to slavery days.

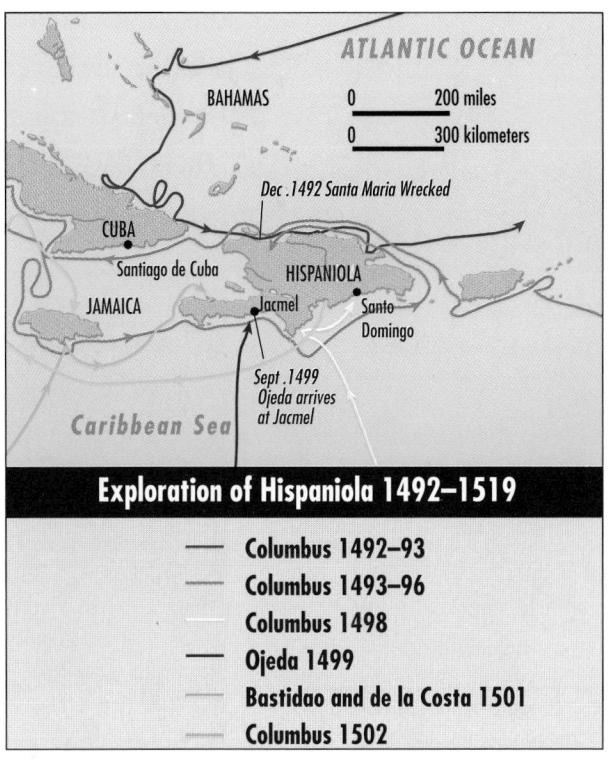

Exploration of Hispaniola 1492–1519

— Columbus 1492–93
— Columbus 1493–96
— Columbus 1498
— Ojeda 1499
— Bastidao and de la Costa 1501
— Columbus 1502

The wreck of the *Santa Maria* on the coast of Hispaniola

sent forty-four sailors ashore where he thought they would be safe. He promised to return and rescue them. The men quickly built a little fort called La Navidad. Before he sailed away, Columbus changed the name Ayiti to Española, or Hispaniola, which means "Little Spain."

Upon his arrival home, he was greeted as a hero. Almost immediately, he outfitted another expedition, consisting of 17 ships and 1,500 men. On his return, Columbus discovered that his stranded crew from the first voyage had been killed by the Arawaks. La Navidad was in ruins. Columbus established another settlement eastward along the coast at Isabela. He put his brother, Bartolme, in charge of colonizing the island. The heavily armed Bartolme and his soldiers quickly killed off the native population.

Columbus's crew destroyed many of the villages.

Slaves were badly treated by the Spanish in Santo Domingo.

Spain claimed all of Hispaniola but actually only colonized the eastern portion of the island over the next hundred years. They called this claim Santo Domingo. By the early 1600s, French settlers had also settled on the island. They established farms and villages on the northern coast. In 1664, Louis XIV gave this area to the French West India Company even though he had no right to give them that land.

It was not until the Treaty of Ryswick in 1697 that the Spanish officially ceded, or gave, the western half of Hispaniola to the French. The name of the French colony became Saint-Domingue, while the Spanish side remained Santo Domingo. In those early

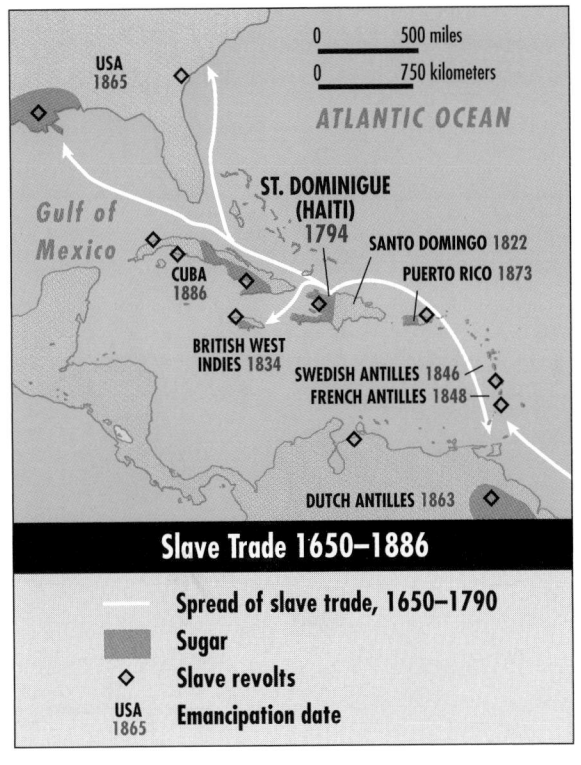

0 — 500 miles
0 — 750 kilometers

ATLANTIC OCEAN

USA 1865

Gulf of Mexico

ST. DOMINIGUE (HAITI) 1794

SANTO DOMINGO 1822
PUERTO RICO 1873

CUBA 1886

BRITISH WEST INDIES 1834

SWEDISH ANTILLES 1846
FRENCH ANTILLES 1848

DUTCH ANTILLES 1863

Slave Trade 1650–1886

— Spread of slave trade, 1650–1790
◻ Sugar
◇ Slave revolts
USA 1865 Emancipation date

years, the French grew indigo, a valuable plant that produces a vibrant blue dye. But they exhausted the soil with this crop and turned to the more profitable sugarcane. The French brought thousands of African slaves to work on their sprawling plantations. Eventually, the blacks outnumbered the whites by ten-to-one.

A Turbulent Time

This was indeed a turbulent time around the world. With the success of the French Revolution in 1789, words such as democracy, republic, and freedom had filtered back to Hispaniola. The white planters born on the island were called creoles. They were determined to be represented in the new national assembly in France. But these full-blood whites did not want to share power with free people of mixed race, or the mulattos (mul-AT-toes). The white

The conditions for slaves led to a rebellion.

Mulattos and Free Blacks

Affranchis is the French word for the mulattos and free blacks in Haiti who led the revolt against France. Among the great Affranchis leaders were Vincent Oge and Jean-Baptiste Chavannes. Unable to secure their rights by diplomacy, they led four hundred Affranchis in the first doomed revolt. The two men were eventually captured and killed. Their heroic efforts lay the foundation for the next round of revolutionary action that took place shortly afterwards.

creoles also ignored the mulattos' requests for seats in the island assembly.

In the meantime, black slaves heard about the French Revolution. The slaves eagerly joined forces with the mulattos and a bloody rebellion broke out in 1791. Fleeing their burning plantations, thousands of whites and loyal slaves abandoned the island. Many went to New Orleans, Louisiana. Their creativity and culture quickly contributed to making that city one of North America's most cosmopolitan communities.

The Hispaniola revolt was led by the Frenchmen Toussaint L'Ouverture, Jean Jacques Dessalines, and Henri Christophe. They soon gained control of French-speaking Saint-Domingue. In 1795, the Spanish gave up their claim to Santo Domingo, turning it over to the French. L'Ouverture then invaded and conquered this territory. With his victory, he set up a government and declared all the slaves free. Although he did not declare independence from France, he frightened the authorities. In 1802, 25,000 French soldiers were sent to put down the rebellion. Against such firepower, the mulattos and the former slaves were soon defeated. Although he was promised safety, L'Ouverture was captured and sent to France where he died in prison.

Yet the French success was short-lived. English warships menaced the surrounding seas, threatening to cut off supplies. Disease deci-

Toussaint L'Ouverture

Jean-Jacques Dessalines

mated the French army. Subsequently, the French withdrew from Hispaniola in 1804. This left the rebels in total control. They turned back to the original Indian name of the island, Haiti, as the name for their new country.

Emperor Assassinated

With L'Ouverture's death, Jean Jacques Dessalines declared himself emperor for life. He called himself Jacques I. He was assassinated in 1806, after which followed several years of political turmoil. Out of the confusion, two separate states emerged. Haiti in the north was ruled by Henri Christophe, or Henri I. The south retained the name of Santo Domingo and was ruled by Alexandre Petion as a republican state.

This did not bring peace. Many different rulers were in both parts of the island over the next few years. Some called themselves emperors. Others were presidents. In this power vacuum, the Spanish returned and seized Santo Domingo. The Treaty of Paris in 1814 allowed the Spanish claim. In the 1820s, however, Haiti reconquered the Spanish half of the island, ruling it for twenty-four years. Keeping its Spanish language, though, Santo Domingo became a separate nation in 1844. Its new name was the Dominican Republic.

A Troubled Haiti

For the next fifty years, internal troubles continued to plague Haiti. The country could not pay its international debts. So, in the early 1900s, the National City Bank of New York took over the National

Bank of Haiti. The bank was concerned about its assets and convinced the United States government that help was needed. The United States also feared that European countries would interfere in the island country's affairs. As a result, United States marines occupied Haiti in 1915. Order was restored, but it came at a price. Haitians had little control over their own destiny as a country, because the North Americans administered the Haitian government and economy.

By 1934, order was restored and United States president Herbert Hoover withdrew the troops. Although the United States had been in Haiti for such a long time, Haiti was still as poor and ill-prepared for the future as when the troops came. Thousands of Haitians emigrated to find jobs. Many went to the neighboring Dominican Republic, but there was still hatred between both of those countries. In 1937, more than 10,000 Haitian workers were massacred in the Dominican Republic by mobs fearing for their own jobs.

A popular Haitian leader named Dusmarsais Estimé came to power in 1946. However, because he instituted many reforms,

The United States occupied Haiti in 1915.

Estimé was deposed by conservative soldiers in a military takeover. It wasn't until 1957, when Dr. François Duvalier was elected president and assumed dictatorial powers, that Haiti had more than a few consecutive years of stable government.

François Duvalier was a country doctor who was admired by Haitians when he was elected. At first, it seemed that Duvalier wanted to help his people. But that impression did not last long. Duvalier wanted more and more power. He became known as Papa Doc. He filled the jails and killed many of his political opponents. He had a private army called the Tontons Macoutes (ton-ton ma-KUTS). In Creole, the word means bogeymen. Anyone brave enough to complain was beaten or killed. Duvalier also used threats of voodoo as well as violence to keep his people in check.

Dusmarsais Estimé

In 1964, Duvalier took the title of President-for-Life. To protect his family interests, he amended the constitution to allow him to nominate his successor. Duvalier immediately named his nineteen-year-old son, Jean-Claude, to be president after his death. Therefore, when Duvalier died April 1971, young Jean-Claude became leader. He took the title as the Dignified Heir. He immediately was nicknamed Baby Doc.

Nothing improved under Jean-Claude Duvalier's administration and there were street demonstrations. He only allowed his supporters to run for office. He closed all the schools and universities and put tight restrictions on the media. Duvalier gave his police and army the power to do almost anything they wanted. The disturbances became so

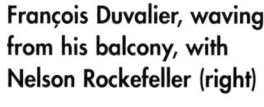

François Duvalier, waving from his balcony, with Nelson Rockefeller (right)

Members of the Tontons Macoutes

Jean-Claude Duvalier became the leader of Haiti after his father's death in 1971.

Haitians standing in line to vote for a new constitution

widespread, however, that Duvalier and his family eventually fled Haiti and went to France in 1986. He took most of the country's treasury with him. An army general and a military-civilian cabinet were left in charge. Many friends of the Duvalier family, called the Dinosaurs, remained in office. This caused additional turmoil.

A new constitution was instituted in March 1987, and a presidential election scheduled for November. Yet, the election had to be called off because remnants of the old Tontons Macoutes were still killing or scaring governmental opponents.

Aristide—A Popular Figure

What followed were several more years of bumbling new governments. One of the leaders of a reform movement was Fr. Jean-Bertrand Aristide. Aristide was a popular figure among the Haitian poor. He was a fiery preacher who encouraged the government and the Roman Catholic Church to remember that their responsibility was to help the people. Aristide wanted a government representing all Haiti's citizens.

After Aristide's election, several army officers did not like the result. They staged a coup, seizing control of the presidential palace in September 1991. Aristide was forced into exile in the United

Father Aristide

Fr. Jean-Bertrand Aristide was born on July 15, 1953, in the village of Port-Salut in southwestern Haiti. His father died shortly after his birth, so Aristide, his mother, and older sister moved to Port-au-Prince. His grandfather encouraged him to study as much as possible. Aristide entered the seminary and was ordained a Roman Catholic priest in 1982.

Aristide gradually became more and more active in politics. He was concerned about the nation's poverty and often spoke out against the government for ignoring the people's problems. For this, Aristide was often threatened and sometimes beaten by the Tontons Macoutes, but he kept protesting. He was convinced to run for president in 1990. One of his mottoes was *makout pa ladan* ("the struggle against corruption"). Aristide was elected by two-thirds of the votes.

States. Tens of thousands of other Haitians fled the country in makeshift boats. Many drowned. All were eventually repatriated, or sent back, to Haiti by the United States.

Blockade Attempted

The international community tried to get the new military rulers to allow Aristide to come back. After all, he had been legitimately elected. An embargo, or a blockade of goods, was attempted. The world hoped this would force the generals to listen. But they did not pay any attention. Oil and other essential goods were too easily smuggled into Haiti across the border with the Dominican Republic. Rich Haitians could easily hop on a jet and fly to France or visit the United States to buy whatever they wanted.

Search for Freedom

A trickle of Haitian refugees in the late 1980s grew into a flood after the military coup in 1991. The desperate Haitians tried to escape their country by sailing away on anything that could float. More than 10,000 persons were taken into custody by the U.S. Coast Guard.

The United States took many of the refugees to special camps at its naval base in Guantanamo, Cuba, or to Panama. The United States said the refugees were not eligible to come to the mainland because they were not political refugees.

Forty black members of the U.S. Congress objected to the repatriation and worked hard to change government policy. Even though a small number of Haitians were eventually sent to safety in several Latin and South American countries, other nations refused them.

The United States then tried to encourage those in Guantanamo to return voluntarily to Haiti. Most refused, so the United States forcibly removed them. By the end of 1995, all these "boat people" had been returned to Haiti.

Children being housed at a U.S. naval base (above)

Many refugees had to return to Haiti. (right)

For months, the United Nations and Organization of American States (OAS) tried to negotiate Aristide's return. They were eventually successful. Under the agreement, the embargo was to be lifted and Aristide given the authority to appoint a new prime minister. He was to be allowed to come back to Haiti.

Food was scarce during the embargo.

Former U.S. President Jimmy Carter helped with a compromise.

But back in Haiti, political violence continued. A group of thugs called the attaches terrorized anyone supporting Aristide's return. The Haitian minister of justice and at least eighty other politically active Haitians were assassinated. Fearing the growing danger, many countries closed down their embassies and evacuated their staffs.

In May 1994, the United Nations tried again to force the illegitimate Haitian government to end the standoff and tightened the embargo. Air links to the country were cut back. A multinational force was prepared to invade Haiti. The invasion was narrowly averted when former U.S. president Jimmy Carter negotiated a compromise settlement. In exchange for calling off the embargo and the invasion, the Haitians were to allow the United Nations troops into the country—all to ease the transition back to civilian rule.

Aristide's Return

That autumn, Aristide returned as a hero and continued his term as president of the country. The generals left the country, after being bribed by the United States to leave. Aristide formed a new government and instituted many reforms. Several thousand troops and police from nearby Caribbean nations and the United States kept an eye on the volatile situation.

By 1996, the political situation in Haiti had stabilized and democratic institutions were reestablished. New elections peacefully brought a fifty-two-year-old agronomist, Rene Préval, to the presidency. Préval was sworn in on February 7, 1996. However, multinational troops remained on duty to make sure the peace continued.

As the country moves into the twenty-first century, the Haitian people wonder what is next in their long history of political turmoil. They hope that the path will be much easier now.

Aristide came back to Haiti as a hero.

A crowd cheering Aristide's return

Governmental Ups and Downs

Ruling Haiti has never been a guarantee of secure employment. Since the founding of the country, there have been two emperors, one king, forty civilian presidents, three military presidents, two provisional presidents, and one prime minister. There have also been nine provisional governments headed by either a military or civilian council. Only seven presidents retired on their own. One of these, Jean-Bertrand Aristide, had to return from exile to finish his term.

I T HAS ALSO BEEN DANGEROUS TO HEAD THE GOVERNMENT. An emperor and one president were assassinated, a king committed suicide, one prime minister was forced to resign, six presidents died in office, one was blown up in his palace, nine were ousted and exiled, six others were simply overthrown, two resigned and were exiled, and eight others simply quit before their term of office was over. In the late 1980s through the mid-1990s, Haiti had twelve different governments during a six-year period. Presidents came and went as through a revolving door. The military regularly interfered with the running of the country.

However, with the reinstatement of President Aristide in 1994 and the subsequent peaceful election of his successor Rene Préval, Haitians hoped for political peace in their future.

Constitution Is Law

As in Canada and the United States, the Haitian constitution is the basic law of the land. Since its founding, the country has had twenty-two constitutions. The first was put into effect on May 20,

Rene Préval

Port-au-Prince: Did You Know This?

Haiti's capital is the sprawling city of Port-au-Prince. It is located on the narrow, flat Cul-de-Sac plain on southwestern coast of Hispaniola. The city is named after the sailing ship, *Prince*, which was one of the first vessels to visit the natural harbor near where the city would be laid out. The French *Port-au-Prince* means "Port of Prince" in English.

Port-au-Prince's official founding is marked as November 26, 1749. The king of France declared it the capital of the French colony of Saint-Domingue in 1770. Its founder, Charles Brunier, was the marquis of Larnage. He was the colony's governor-general from 1737 to 1746.

Today, about 750,000 people reside in Port-au-Prince. They live in homes ranging from shacks to mansions. The capital's presidential palace, the White House (above), looks over the city from a wide promenade. Other governmental offices are nearby.

Port-au-Prince: Facts and Figures

Population (1995 est.): 752,600 (1,255,078 metropolitan area)
Ethnic Breakdown: 93% Black; 5% Mulatto; 1% White; 1% Arab
Year Founded: November 26, 1749
Founder: Charles Brunier
Altitude: Sea level
Average Temperature: 94°F (34°C) in July; 87°F (31°C) in January
Average Annual Precipitation: 49 inches (124 cm)

1805, by Jean-Jacques Dessalines. The current constitution was written in 1987 and copied articles from both the French and United States constitutions. The Haitian document establishes the government as a republic, consisting of nine departments (*departements*). Departments are similar to a province in Canada or a state in the United States. The nine departments are West (Ouest), North (Nord), Northeast (Nord-Est), Northwest (Nord-Ouest), Artibonite (Artibonite), Central (Centre), Southeast (Sud-Est), South (Sud), and Grand' Anse.

Each department consists of several districts (*arrondissements*). There are forty-one of these districts throughout Haiti. The districts are further divided into communal sections, sometimes called urban centers. These are the country's smallest administrative units. They consist of a city, its suburbs, and a rural area around it.

Almost two million people live in the five districts of the Western department, making it the largest in Haiti. One district in the Western department is that of Port-au-Prince, consisting of six communes. These communes include the capital city of Port-au-Prince, along with Delmas, Petionville,

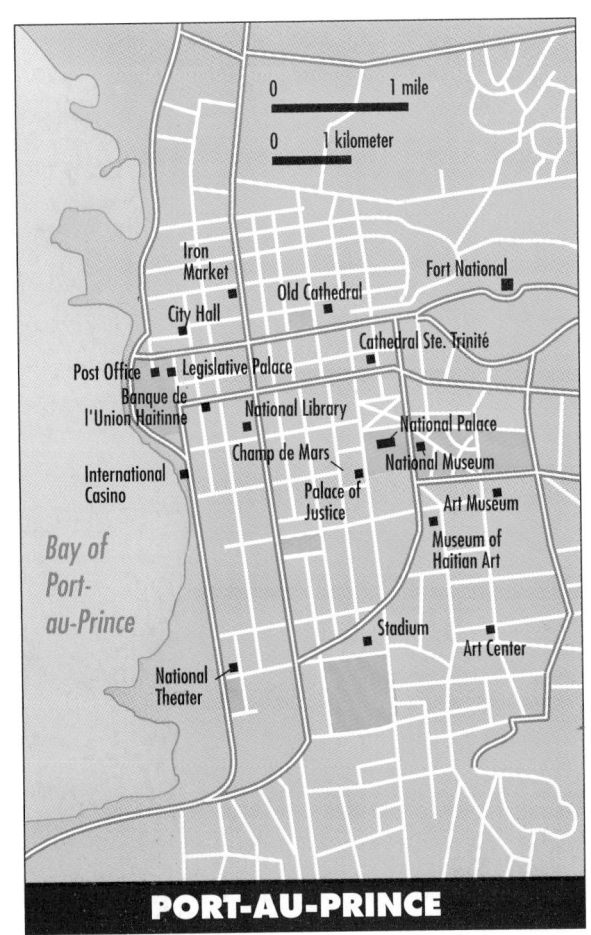

PORT-AU-PRINCE

City Hall in Port-au-Prince

Jean-Jacques Dessalines—The Father of Haiti

Jean-Jacques Dessalines was born a slave on a plantation in 1758 and ran away to freedom when he was thirty-three. Dessalines became the main lieutenant of revolutionary hero Toussaint L'Ouverture in the great slave rebellion that led to Haiti's independence. When L'Ouverture was captured and sent to prison in France, Dessalines became general-in-chief of the revolution. He was a brave soldier, once threatening to blow up a fort rather than surrender it to the French. He led the army of former slaves in several major victories over the French army.

On January 1, 1804, Dessalines proclaimed the independence of the colony and gave it the official name of Haiti. He was crowned emperor but was assassinated in another revolt in 1806. Dessalines is remembered as the Father of Haiti.

President Aristide (center) with U.S. President Bill Clinton (right) and U.N. Secretary-General Boutros Boutros-Ghali (left)

Kenscoff, Gressier, and Carrefour. Every commune is governed by a three-member municipal council elected for four years. The head of the council is a mayor, who also holds office for four years.

The president is the head of state, holding office for five years. A president can be elected for only one more term. The president's duties include representing the government in international matters and giving overall direction to the country. The president also chooses a prime minister from the majority political party in the parliament. The nomination must be approved by parliament.

The prime minister's job is to organize and run the government's day-to-day operations. The prime minister heads a cabinet of other ministers. They are responsible for: agriculture; education; finance and economics; foreign affairs; industry and commerce; information; interior and defense; justice; planning; public works, transport, and telecommunications; and social affairs.

Governmental Agencies

There are also several independent governmental agencies. These function as arms of the government and are a mix of financial, business, and social institutions. They include the Central Bank of Haiti, Haitian electrical and telecommunications companies, an auto insurance agency, the airport authority, the Port-au-Prince sewer and water service, a national water service, a flour-milling company and a cement plant, printing services, the national pension and retirement agency, and several business development and investment agencies. There is also an agency overseeing retail stores and a Haitian National Lottery. The long arm of the Haitian government extends deeply into almost all aspects of Haitian life.

Haiti's parliament consists of two houses. One is a eighty-three-member Chamber of Deputies and the other is the twenty-seven-member Senate. One deputy is elected from each of eighty-three electoral dis-

There is a national water service, but running water is rare.

National Anthem of Haiti

"Song of Dessalines" (*La Dessalinienne*), music by Nicolas Geffrard, words by Justin L'herisson

I

For our Country,
For our Ancestors,
Let's march in unity.
In our ranks, no traitors,
We shall be the sole masters of our
    land.
Let's march in unity,
For our Country, for our Ancestors.
Let's march in unity,
For our Country, for our Ancestors.

II

For our Founding Fathers,
For our Nation,
Let's happily plough,
When the field bears fruit
The soul is strengthened,
Let's happily plough
For our Founding Fathers,
For our Nation
Let's happily plough,
For our Founding Fathers,
For our Nation.

III

To Our Country
And to our Forefathers
Let's be sons.
Free, strong and prosperous,

We will always be brothers.
Let's be sons,
To our Country,
And to our Forefathers,
Let's be sons,
To our Country,
And to our Forefathers.

IV

For our Founding Fathers,
For our Nation,
O God of the doughty knights!
Under your endless protection
Take our rights, our life.
O God of the doughty knights!
For our Founding Fathers,
For our Nation,
O God of the doughty knights!
For our Founding Fathers,
For our Nation.

V

For our Flag, for our Nation,
Dying is beautiful.
Our past is shouting to us:
"Harden your soul for battle."
Dying is beautiful,
For our Flag, for our Nation,
Dying is beautiful,
For our Flag, for our Nation.

tricts and serves for four years. Three senators from each department are elected for six-year terms. Voting for senators takes place every two years, with one-third of the seats up for re-election each time.

The Haitian Senate in session

In the pre-Aristide days in Haitian politics, the key to holding power was control of the army and police. Whoever had support of the security forces usually stayed in power, at least for a time. Sometimes, various dictators

Haiti's National Flag

The Haitian flag was created on May 18, 1803. Revolutionary leaders Jean-Jacques Dessalines and Alexandre Petion tore off the white middle section of the old blue, white, and red French flag. They joined the blue and red pieces, symbolizing the unity of mulattos and blacks. Seamstress Catherine Flon then sewed the pieces together to make a banner for the new country. However, in 1964, dictator Francois Duvalier replaced that flag with a black-and-red striped flag of his own design. When his son, Jean-Claude Duvalier, fled Haiti for France in 1986, the country's original flag was restored.

Today's Haitian flag shows horizontal blue-and-red colors, with the blue on top and red underneath. The Haitian coat-of-arms is a white square center panel.

This national emblem contains a palm, the tree of freedom. The tree is topped by a stocking cap symbolizing liberty. Flags are on both sides of the tree. Two cannons are above a banner bearing the motto "Unity Makes Strength" (*L'Union Fait la Force*).

A new graduating class of the police force

had their own private armies as well, such as the feared Tontons Macoutes under the Duvaliers. When President Aristide returned from exile in 1994, there were 7,300 men and women in the Haiti defense force. He reduced the troop level to about 1,500 uniformed officers. Aristide also formed a new 4,000-member civilian police force separate from the army. Several high-ranking police officers from the United States and other countries helped train these new police officers. The international advisors attempted to make the police more responsible to the people.

Napoleonic Code

Haitian law is based on the French Napoleonic Code. This was the first modern organized body of law. It was enacted by Emperor Napoleon I in 1804. The code was his interpretation of old Roman law or civil law that dominated Europe for centuries. Civil law is still the major body of law in the world, outside of England and its former colonies, including the United States and Canada.

Haiti's courts of appeal and civil courts are located in the capital of Port-au-Prince and the three provincial capitals of Gonaïves, Cap Haitien, and Port de Paix. In addition to these courts, each commune has a magistrate's court for minor offenses such as shoplifting and speeding. Judges for the Supreme Court and the courts of appeal are appointed by the president for terms of ten years. The Supreme Court gives the final decision in any legal questions.

Ensuring a separate, honest judicial system was a goal of the 1990s reform movement. Too often in the past, judges were dishonest and corrupt. People often had to give them bribes. Under the constitution today, the Senate may even take over the powers of a High Court of Justice. Under this rule, a president and governmental ministers can be tried for crimes such as treason or abuse of power.

The Supreme Court makes final decisions on legal questions.

Haitians sometimes take justice into their own hands, in spite of the legal system in place.

Because they could not trust the courts, Haitians often took the law into their own hands. This was a process called *dechoukaj* or uprooting. Arson, beatings, and lynchings were common. Necklacing was another act of revenge. With this, a gasoline-soaked tire was place around a victim's neck and set on fire. The person usually died.

Presidents Aristide and Préval have tried to stop all this violence. Haitian lawyers, judges, and court officials are undergoing better training so abuses will not occur again.

But habits and suspicions die hard. Outside observers agree that violence and lawlessness are deeply rooted in Haiti. The Haitian constitution has many articles asserting civil rights and justice for all. But no leader, whether democratically elected or not, can ensure respect for human rights until there is a rule of law, civilian control, and an honest court system.

A U.N. officer keeping the peace between the crowd and the police

Haiti's Rock 'n' Roll Economy

From the beginning, Haiti's economy has been unstable. Its leaders allowed graft and corruption to flourish. The country's natural and economic resources have not been managed well. As a result, Haiti has long been one of the poorest countries in the world. It is still the poorest in the Western Hemisphere.

70

OFTEN, HAITI'S PRESIDENTS and their cronies have grown rich from the financial help that poured into the country. The money seldom trickled down to the people it was supposed to serve. This was especially true during the Cold War of the 1950s and 1960s, when Western Europe and the United States were opposed to the Communist policies of the Soviet Union, enforced in Eastern Europe. It was not uncommon for desperately hungry Haitians to sell their blood to companies that shipped it to hospitals overseas. They also sold cadavers, which are dead bodies, that were used for medical research.

Haiti remains one of the poorest countries in the world.

At this time, the corrupt Haitian government often played up the fact that it was anticommunist. Since Communist-run Cuba is so close to Haiti, the United States sent money to help Haiti. Unfortunately, with all of Haiti's corruption, most of these funds went toward building lighted tennis courts, swimming pools, and mansions for Haiti's military commanders, the police chiefs, and the politicians.

A Continuing Decline

The downhill slide of the 1990s was a continuation of a decline under the thirty-year regimes of dictators François Duvalier and his

son, Jean-Claude. The collapse of the Haitian economy went even faster when the military overthrew President Aristide. Protesting his ouster, the Organization of American States set up an international trade embargo against Haiti. (An embargo is a restriction on commerce imposed by law.) This action, along with a three-year suspension of international aid, was a serious blow to Haiti's already feeble economy.

The wealthy in Haiti enjoy beach clubs.

Opposite: **Many Haitians live in shacks such as these.**

One of Jean-Claude Duvalier's many beach houses

Rising Inflation

Inflation rose during the military takeover in the early 1990s. Inflation is when prices of goods rise quickly. For instance, a pound of vegetables might double in price from one day to the next. This economic situation certainly made it hard for families, because salaries did not keep up with the rising prices. People were afraid to put money in banks because it lost value in a savings account.

Even toward the end of the 1990s, almost half the Haitian population do not have a full-time paying job. Those who are lucky enough to have jobs are paid very poorly. The average yearly wage of the typical Haitian city dweller is barely 15 to 16.50 groudes a day. That is equal to earning only $3 to $3.30 a day in United States dollars. Many Haitians make less than $500 a year. However, a few Haitian business people and politicians remain very wealthy. The gap between these people and the ordinary citizens is dramatic.

Kids in Haiti do what they can to help their mothers and fathers. From an early age, most children work on their family garden plot, tend the livestock and take produce to market. Others are shoeshine boys in Port-au-Prince, earning only a few centimes for a polish. They attract customers

Some Haitians work in factories.

A worker making a living in a quarry

Money Facts

The basic monetary unit in Haiti is the gourde. The value of one gourde is equal to about six cents in United States currency. Banknotes are issued in denominations of 1, 2, 5, 10, 50, 100, 250, and 500 gourdes. There are coins, as well. They are minted in 5, 10, 20 and 50 centime (cents) denominations.

Most of the bills and coins carry portraits of Haiti's leaders. Some older money is still in circulation. The face of the late dictator François Duvalier remains on the brown 1 gourde bill and the gray 2 gourde bill. His exiled son Jean-Claude is still on the orange 5 gourde bill and the green 10 gourde note. Haitian liberator Henri Christophe is on the purple 100 gourde bill, with Jean-Jacques Dessalines on the yellow-green 250 gourde banknote.

Children often help out on farms.

by tapping their shoeboxes on the sidewalks. Their clack-clack-clack makes a rhythmic tune.

Others carry visitors' bags or act as guides around the port. Today, young city girls are housekeepers, seamstresses, or work in factories. Working on factory assembly lines is considered a good job. The workers might not make much money, but everything is shared with their families. There is a Haitian proverb that says "working is not easy but you get what you work for."

Exports Tumble

During the years of the military takeover in the early 1990s, the number of exports (goods shipped out of a country) tumbled. Imports (the goods coming in) also dropped because other countries would not trade with Haiti. In addition, investments in new businesses decreased. This made it hard to start new businesses. It was also difficult to keep old, out-of-date equipment running. The system, already in bad shape, broke down.

Sanctions Lifted

The return to power of President Aristide in October 1994 was a blessing. The international sanctions were lifted, setting the stage for a recovery. However, Haiti still has many difficulties. Only a few of the country's roads are paved. There are electrical power outages and a shortage of clean water. The Port-au-Prince harbor is in disrepair so shipping is hindered. Most homes outside Port-au-Prince in the shabby suburbs of Brooklyn and Bel Air do not have electricity, tap water, or telephone service. School kids sometimes take their books outside to study under the dim light of street lamps.

The governments of Aristide and Préval said they were committed to cleaning up the problems of the past. Both presidents eagerly sought foreign investments and bank loans to help get their country moving again. One of the first goals was to help farmers, because about two-thirds of all Haitians work in agriculture. During the military takeover, demand for Haiti's farm goods dropped. Only the export of deliciously sweet mangoes to the United States and Canada continued to be high. More than two million cases of this yellow-red fruit were sent abroad each year.

Other products are slowly making a comeback. Abundant crops of strawberries and other vegetables from the Kenscoff region sell well. The tiny bitter Seville

Paying Debts to France

Haiti was forced to pay back money to France after its revolution. In 1825, King Charles X of France signed an ordinance demanding the money. The ordinance was delivered to Haiti by a fleet of fourteen French warships. This drain on its treasury affected the Haitian economy for more than a century. In order to be recognized as an independent nation, Haiti had to return 150 million francs to white planters who were expelled or fled during the rebellion. In 1996, United States currency, that repayment amount was worth $29,257,446.02.

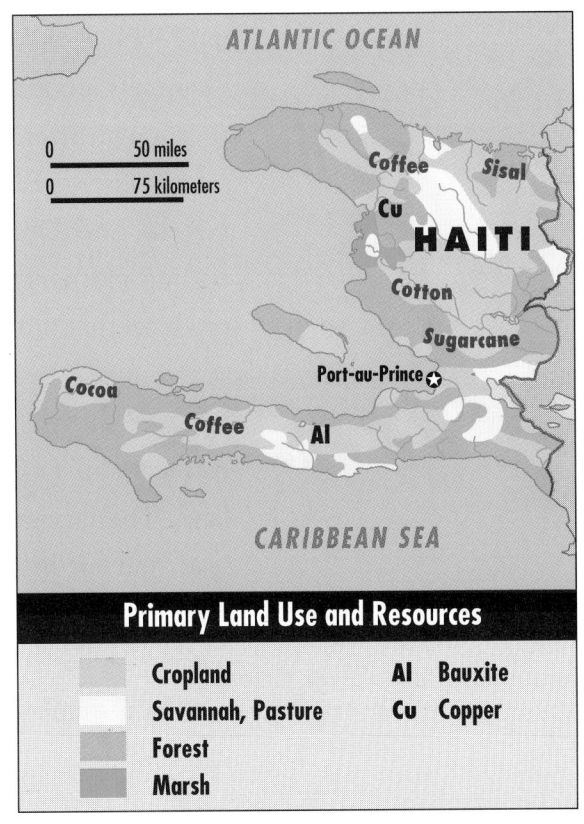

Primary Land Use and Resources

Cropland	Al Bauxite
Savannah, Pasture	Cu Copper
Forest	
Marsh	

Ships unloading at Port-au-Prince

orange also grows in Haiti's favorable climate. Small black Haitian mushrooms, called djon-djons (jon-jons) are rare and expensive. Gourmets around the world pay high prices for a shipment of these tiny fungi. Strong Haitian coffee is grown in the mountains and sold overseas. Rice, sorghum, corn, and sugarcane are also harvested. The United States, Italy, and France are Haiti's major trading partners, receiving almost 90 percent of the agricultural products that are available for sale.

Problems Loom

Farmers still face problems. They work poor, inefficient plots of land. The farmers do not have a lot of money to invest in tools, seed, and fertilizer and it is difficult to get loans. The irrigation system for watering crops has fallen into disrepair. The land is overexploited because of the large population.

On a small scale, however, several international agencies are still trying to help. Some have arranged loan packages for Haitians

starting businesses. One such group is World Concern's Micro-Enterprise Rural Credit Program. Hundreds of families have received backing to help them on their farms, develop food processing companies, and open retail shops. The loans have been repaid 99 percent of the time. The Vermont Partnership for Health, Education, and Environment helps villagers in the town of Dessable. Among its efforts, Partnership staff teach people to use solar ovens. This lessens the amount of firewood being used and saves trees.

Going to market is always a big event for Haitians. Most towns are gathering points for the rural folk. Pipe-smoking Madame Sarahs, a nickname for elderly farm ladies, balance large wicker baskets of produce on their heads. Live chickens and little black pigs, rice and beans, mangoes and bananas, CDs and shoes, chewing gum and shirts, and auto parts and books are offered for sale at the market. A smart shopper can find almost anything in this cross between an outdoor supermarket and a discount mall.

Many women on the way to the market carry produce on their heads.

Farmers face many problems in Haiti.

Bargaining is expected. The market is also always a good place to catch up on the latest gossip and to say hello to friends.

Main Industries

Sugar refining, textile manufacturing, and parts assembly are the main industries in Haiti. Factories are clustered in dusty industrial parks near Port-au-Prince. However, many industries pulled out of the country when the generals marched in. But in the late 1990s, businesses began their slow return when Aristide came back. The lure of cheap Haitian labor remains very attractive to international firms. The companies make a wide range of items from tennis shoes to shirts and electronic components to baseballs.

One possible bright spot on the economic front is the return of tourism. The first cruise ship visited Haiti in 1957, followed by others until the Duvalier dictatorship drove them away. It is hoped that the island's natural beauty, inexpensive craft items, and the friendliness of the people will

The marketplace in Port-au-Prince

A Haitian factory making baseballs

What Haiti Grows, Makes, and Mines

Agriculture

Sugarcane	2,250,000	metric tons
Plantains	272,000	metric tons
Mangoes	230,000	metric tons

Manufacturing

Cement	84,000	metric tons
Essential oils (mostly amyris, neroli, and vetiver)	227	metric tons
Cigarettes	408,000,000	units

Mining

Limestone	220,000	metric tons
Marble	500	cubic meters

Beautiful hotels attract tourists to Haiti.

attract more visitors. Now that the repressive regimes are in the past, tourists might feel more comfortable visiting this island nation. But they should not expect all the comforts of home.

Haiti imports about $424 million of goods and products every year. This is far above the $135 million of goods shipped out of the country. This situation is called a trade imbalance, a problem when more goods come in than go out. The United States, the Netherland Antilles, Japan, France, Canada, and Germany are the largest import partners. Washing machines, oil, food, and vehicles are sent to Haiti, along with many other products.

Illicit drugs are also becoming more of a problem. The country has become a transfer point for drug dealers. They fly back and forth to the United States and Europe with cocaine and marijuana. Police from many nations help the Haitians keep track of this traffic and attempt to stop it. Some high-ranking Haitians have been accused of aiding the smugglers and a few have been put in prison. But so much money is made in drugs, it is hard to keep it all under control.

Yet despite all the difficulties in conducting trade, the ordinary Haitian people remain willing and eager to make a difference. They are working hard to pull their country out of its economic mess.

Imported food for sale

Today's Haitians

Most Haitians are descended from the slaves brought to the colony by the French colonizers. At the time of the Haitian war for independence, there were at least 500,000 slaves, 32,000 whites, and 24,000 mulattos on the island. The whites kept the slaves under control by torture and fear. Many terrible punishments were given to slaves who disobeyed or rebelled. Some were stuffed with gunpowder and blown up. Others were buried up to their neck in sand and their faces covered with honey to attract insects. Sometimes, hot wax was poured in their ears.

THE SLAVES GOT THEIR REVENGE DURING THEIR REVOLUTION against the planters. Massacres and torture were commonplace. Atrocities were conducted by both sides. After the revolt, few whites remained in Haiti.

Today, more than 95 percent of the 6,647,00 Haitians trace their heritage through the slave era to black Africa. Another 4 percent are mulattos. About 1 percent are white and most of these are not native-born Haitians but long-time foreign residents who like Haiti.

A temple honoring the end of slavery at Le Cap

When most of the whites fled after the slave revolution, the mulattos gained power. Under French colonial law, these racially mixed Haitians were free citizens. The planters often sent their mulatto children to France to study. Since they could inherit property, many mulattos were very wealthy. After the revolution, they became the ruling class for a time because of their lighter skin. Anything "European" or white was mistakenly thought to be better than African or black. Even today, this unspoken racial divide exists.

From its very beginning as a nation, Haiti was affected by shades of skin. It did not make any difference that the declarations of independence of the United States and Haiti

Children learn of their history and are proud to be Haitian.

were similar. Politicians overseas were still wary of the Haiti's black leaders. They were afraid of seeing blacks in power, especially since slavery was still legal in many parts of the world including the United States. U.S. president Thomas Jefferson was afraid that Haiti might invade the United States to release the slaves there.

For generations, many Haitians felt it better to be as much like the whites as possible. Being "French" was best. Despite this emphasis on European heritage and light skin, however, some Haitian families respectfully guarded their black African heritage. Anthropologist Jean Price-Mars was one of these people. He was the best known of a long line of authors, diplomats, doctors, and governmental officials. He authored a world-recognized history of Haiti and its folktales called *Thus Spake the Uncle* (*Ainsi Parla l'Oncle*). He wanted his fellow citizens to be proud of their heritage.

The Pan-Africa Movement

The Pan-Africa movement was strong in Haiti in the early 1900s. This was a belief that all good things came from Africa, the mother continent. Haitian writers joined those from Jamaica, Ethiopia, Trinidad, Liberia, and the few other countries with black leaders at that time. Their pride in Africa was very strong. Haitian author

Massillon Coicou continually reminded his fellow citizens that any race "which is ignorant of its origins is doomed." Poets such as Felix Morisseau-Leroy wrote in Creole. He even adapted Greek plays into his native language.

Yet, there are upper-class Haitians with dark skins and lower-class Haitians with light skins. So social standing is judged by other measures, as well. It is also beneficial if a Haitian can trace his or her family back to the leaders of the revolution. Money also makes a big difference. One Haitian proverb says that a poor mulatto is black and a rich black is a mulatto.

Haitians speak a mixture of French and several African dialects called Creole. Creole is considered a language of the lower classes. The educated elite speak French. Often the poorer Haitians cannot understand what their wealthy neighbors are saying, and in turn, the upper classes cannot understand Creole.

Who Lives in Haiti?	
Black	95%
Mulatto	4%
Arab and White	1%

The language in Haiti is a mix of French and several African dialects.

Creole Pronunciation Key

The principal difference between English and Haitian Creole is in how parts of words are stressed. In Creole, the final part of the word is usually emphasized more strongly. Compare the English words "do," "low," "see" and "pay" with some Creole words. Note how the vowels "o," "e" and "a" are stretched out in English as in "doooo," "loooow," "seeee" and "paaaay." Now try pronouncing the Haitian words "dou," "dio," "se" and "pe," with a shorter vowel sound. The lips are not supposed to move on the vowels.

Common Creole Words and Phrases

Good morning	Bon jour
Who are you?	Ki moun ou ye?
Please	Tan pri souple
What's up?	Sa-k pase?
family	fanmi
father	papa
mother	manman
brother	fre
sister	se
grandmother	granme
grandfather	grandpe

Populations of Haiti's Largest Cities

Port-au-Prince	752,600
Cap Haitien	92,122
Gonaïves	63,291
Cayes	36,000

Opposite: **There are some wealthy sections in Port-au-Prince.**

Language Choices

In the rich suburbs of Port-au-Prince, the cooks, nannies, and other hired staff speak rich colorful Creole in the kitchen and garden. But French is the language of choice around the family dinner table. Day-to-day speech is dotted with phrases taken from other cultures, especially English. Often words such as Big Mac and air conditioning are spoken in English. Some words sound much the same. *Amerikin* is American, *adopte* (adoptay) means to adopt, *agrikol* is agriculture, and *egzamen* is exam.

Haitians delight in talking. Their words flow like a soft stream down a mountain slope. Haitians have many proverbs in their rich speech. Elders warn, "*Cause made chaise*" ("You need to sit down to hear a good story"). Some phrases are political, "*Bourik travay chousal galonnin*" ("The poor works while the rich plays"). Others are perceptive, "*Piti pi bone pase anyin*" ("Just a little is better than

Many Haitians enjoy spending time talking to one another.

A typical middle-class neighborhood in Port-au-Prince

nothing at all"). Others are simply fun, *"Tout voum ce do"* ("All sound can be music").

Haiti is one of the most densely populated countries in the world, with more than 600 persons per square mile (238 per sq km). (The U.S. average is about 74 persons per square mile.) The population has risen from about 4 million in the 1950s to more than 7 million in the late 1990s. The country has a difficult time supporting this many people. Some 80 percent of its citizens live in rural areas, with most clustered in the districts near the coast.

In the countryside, heavy work is made lighter by work songs (*combites*). Groups of people help each other put up houses, clear fields, and repair roads. There is usually a lot of singing and chanting. It is like dancing in tune with the hammers and hoes.

At the end of the day, the host family feeds the tired friends who helped them.

The houses in the hills are often made of mud, with thatch or straw roofs. Because it is chilly in the mountains, charcoal stoves heat the houses, which pollutes the air. Few homes have indoor plumbing, except in some of the wealthier resort communities above Port-au-Prince.

Proper sanitation is almost nonexistent in Haiti. Streams and rivers carry off sewage. Mothers might wash their clothes just down the river from a donkey standing knee-deep in the current. Keeping a body length away from wading animals was once thought to be enough to get pure water.

There are usually health problems in the villages, ranging from malnutrition to AIDS. There are also signs of malaria. The average life span of a Haitian is fifty-five years.

A mountain village

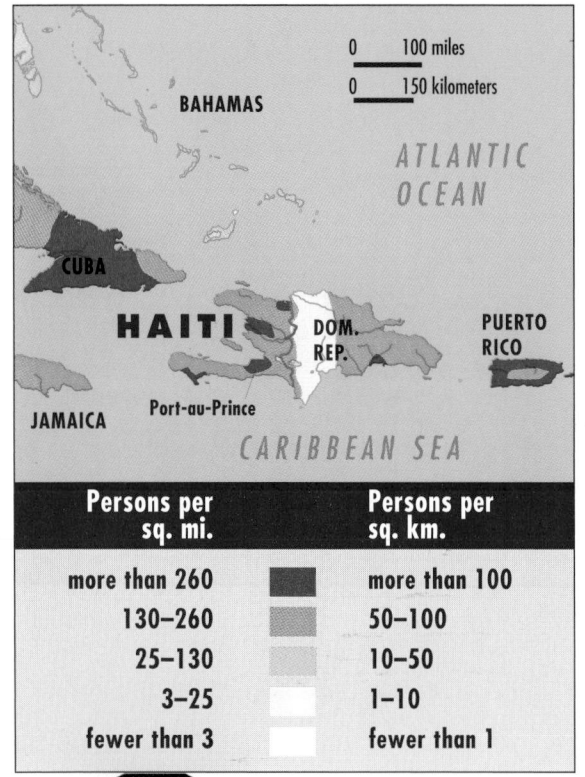

Persons per sq. mi.		Persons per sq. km.
more than 260		more than 100
130–260		50–100
25–130		10–50
3–25		1–10
fewer than 3		fewer than 1

Voodoo practitioners can alleviate many minor health problems by using their healing herbs. Voodoo doctors will encourage patients to get more assistance if necessary. Ordinary Haitians, however, usually cannot afford to pay a medical doctor or are afraid to visit a clinic or hospital. So sick or injured people often do not seek more help.

Because few working telephones are in the outlying areas of Haiti, Haitian peasants depend on word of

mouth, the *telijiol*, to get the latest information. In the past, the *telijiol* has often been more accurate and trustworthy than official government proclamations and the press.

In the cities, there are problems with overcrowding, lack of jobs, and poor sanitation. In the 1970s and 1980s, tens of thousands of Haitians came down from the mountains seeking work. They erected shacks out of tin and boards found in rubbish dumps. While some new housing was built for the poorer people in the tightly packed slums like La Saline in the late 1990s, much remains to be done.

In some areas of Haiti, sanitation is poor.

Opposite: **Some Haitians see medical doctors; others visit voodoo doctors.**

A World of Spirits

The deep thunder of beating drums rolls down from the mountains behind Port-au-Prince. Shadows move swiftly across the ground as evening advances into night. The drums beat in the night air. Crowds dressed in white walk along the dusty roads toward a Haitian voodoo ceremony. Earlier, these same people were at Sunday mass in the local Catholic church. While this might seem odd to an outsider, the ordinary Haitian has feet planted in two different religious worlds. But because both worlds are of the spirit, it all makes sense to them.

T HE BLACK SLAVES BROUGHT TO HAITI were displaced persons. They were Senegalese, Aradas, Yoruba, Fidas, Fanti, Ibo, and dozens of other tribes. All were ripped away from their Dahomey, Ashanti, and Mandingo empires and other African home-lands. But they brought their rituals, music, language, and gods to the Caribbean islands. Whenever possible, the slaves ran away or rebelled. They probably met fugitive Indians in the mountains. From this mix, a single religion called voodoo evolved. In the dialects of West Africa, the word voodoo means spirit. Today, voodoo has become political. Some Haitian intellec-tuals say that practicing voodoo proclaims their country's independence. It keeps the outside world from interfering with Haiti.

Justin Chrystome Dorsainvil

Justin Chrystome Dorsainvil was born in Port-au-Prince in 1880. He studied medicine, taught school, and worked in the department of education. Although he died in 1942, his writings on Haiti are still considered influential. He was one of the first educated Haitians to emphasize the importance of voodoo. Dorsainvil called voodoo part of the ethnic capital, or spiritual treasury, of his fellow Haitians. He traced this back to their African roots. "I am an African whom historical acci-dent has displaced from his original milieu (or place)," he wrote.

Beliefs Merge

For years after the slave revolution, Catholic priests struggled to convince Haitians not to follow voodoo. Yet African and Christian traditions are not all that different under the surface. It was easy for the slaves to blend many beliefs and traditions into their own brand of religion. Both Christianity and voodoo have baptism, or ritual purification. They both had a main god that created all people. Christian saints became voodoo spirits. For instance St. Patrick dri-ving the snakes from Ireland became Damballah, the voodoo

serpent deity. Today, few Haitians think there is much problem in going to Christian services and then practicing voodoo.

Yet voodoo remains primarily a religion of the poor. Elite, wealthy, educated Haitians claim to know little of voodoo's intricate services or the meanings of its symbols. Belief in voodoo marks one more class division between the country's citizens. In Haiti's early years, the mulattos and the first rulers of the country denounced voodoo as uncivilized. In their minds, it was un-European. And after all, to be European was to be accepted as a legitimate nation by the wider white world.

As in other religions, voodoo is based on certain principles, with its own set of rites. There are ministers or priests to perform the rites. The voodoo priest is the *houngan*. A priestess is a *mambo*. But unlike a Catholic priest, the houngan's religious authority is more informal. There is no centralized voodoo church, with all its rules and a power structure. A priest, however, is answerable to his bishops and the pope. In addition, one of the primary duties of the houngan and mambo is treating sickness and injury, usually with herbs. So the voodoo practitioners could be considered doctors, as well.

In voodoo, the saints and God of Christianity are translated into *loas*, or ancestral spirits. The loas are rather similar to the gods of Greek and Roman mythology, because they also represent

A Catholic mass

Opposite: **In this voodoo ceremony, Haitians walk into muddy water to free themselves from *loas*, the voodoo spirits.**

A painting of a loa on a voodoo temple

aspects of nature. The loas live in water and trees. They act as intermediaries between the main voodoo god, the Gran Met, and the houngans and mambos. Singing and dancing in a voodoo ceremony causes a trance in which the loas can communicate with the houngan and mambo.

These elaborate ceremonies are held in places called *hounfors*, which can be sheds, houses, or openings in the forest. Inside the sacred area is an altar, called either the *pe* or *sobagui*. Elaborately sewn flags provide background color. These flags can be so beautiful that they are considered art and have been hung in galleries such as the Fowler Museum in Los Angeles, California. The hounfors floor or the ground is covered with cornmeal, soot, brick dust or coffee grounds. This powdery material is then swirled about in fragile, intricate designs that represent voodoo symbols.

Voodoo!

Voodoo doctors in Haiti use plants and other items for treatment. A spiderweb is placed over a cut to help stop bleeding. Peppermint tea helps to keep a sick child from throwing up. Chewing parsley root clears a raspy voice.

The patient always pays, but it might be a chicken or a goat instead of money. By giving a gift, the Haitian feels that something good is returned to the person who did the original service. Haitians do not trust anyone who does something for nothing. This is why a free clinic in Haiti is sometimes not a success. "What value is such a place," the Haitians ask.

Voodoo Flags

Haitian voodoo flags are made of satin or silk and embroidered with sequins, beads, and iridescent seed pearls. The symbols are taken from African, Roman Catholic, Masonic, and Arawak Indian traditions. The banners contain the same symbols as the floor drawings, but in more detail. These flags are important in many of the voodoo ceremonies.

At the beginning of a ceremony, the banners are taken from their secret hiding place, and are brought forward into the candlelight by hounsis. These are apprentice mambos who are accompanied by a man carrying a machete, a large knife used on Haitian farms. The hounsis wave the flags to call the loas. The flags also signify the changing from the real to the spirit world. This allows the loas to appear and "mount," or possess, the voodoo participants.

The altar is sacred in a voodoo ceremony.

Voodoo has substituted its own symbols for those of Christianity. In place of Virgin Mary is a being called Erzulie Freda. She is the loa of love. Bondieu is the head loa and is very powerful. Another strong loa is Baron Samedi, who dresses in black and is lord of the underworld. Haitian dictator Francois Duvalier used this loa to frighten his people into obeying him.

Voodoo is a mixture of fear and joy. There are animal sacrifices, spells, pins stuck into dolls, and soulless creatures called zombies

A mixture of Catholicism and voodoo, as Haitians celebrate All Saints' Day and the ceremony of the Gedes, the voodoo spirits of death

who roam the world. It is easy for the outsider to concentrate on the scary parts of voodoo. But voodoo also celebrates beauty and life, as well as death. Voodoo simply admits that no one can escape death.

The function of voodoo is to serve the gods. This is not black magic, according to voodoo practioners. Black magic wants to manipulate the gods and make them serve people. This is very dangerous, they agree, because black magic can turn on you and destroy you.

Even with voodoo, the Catholic Church retains its importance. Mass is sung in Creole. Drums are used at church services. However, sometimes bishops sided with the upper classes during the reigns of dictators. On the other hand, the parish priest usually supported the poor and often spoke out for them.

During Duvalier's harsh regime, the Church led many of the protests against him. This is one of the reasons that Fr. Jean-Bertrand Aristide became so popular. The ordinary people knew he was a priest on their side. He did not give even up when he was threatened or attacked by the police. Eventually, Aristide was elected president of Haiti.

Church Persecuted

Because of its outspoken concern for the rights of the people, the Church was persecuted. Many clergymen and nuns were killed. The message of love was taken outside church buildings. A movement called Ti Leglis (Little Church in Creole) made the Catholic Church part of the people's daily lives. People were taught to read. Church officials organized clothing drives, operated food pantries,

Religions of Haiti*

80%	Roman Catholic
16%	Protestant
4%	Other

*Most Haitians practice some form of voodoo in conjunction with their professed religion.

and set up rural medical clinics. The Church-run Radio Soleil actively gave voice to dissenters. Its programs were in Creole so the poor could understand what was being said.

While the Roman Catholic Church is the official religion of Haiti, there are also several Protestant denominations in Haiti. Among them are the Episcopalian, Church of the Latter Day Saints, and the Baptist. But only 16 percent of the population follows any of these denominations.

Only a few Jews live in Haiti today. There are plenty of churches but no synagogues. Over the centuries, however, Jews have lived and worked in Haiti.

The cathedral at Port-au-Prince

Haitians can belong to any religion they wish, a right guaranteed by the country's constitution. But there are numerous superstitions.

Spirits, for example, roam the Haitian countryside. Watch out for *cochons-sans-poils*, the white pigs without hair. These evil creatures slip in and out of the forest and are usually seen at crossroads. It is said they will capture your soul if they see you. To protect yourself, take some dirt in your left hand and hold it against your forehead. Say "Earth." Then place your hand on your chest. Say "In earth." Then move your hand against the left shoulder and say, "To earth return." Finally, put your hand on your right shoulder and say "Thou art dust and to dust thou shalt return."

Another monster is called Little Casket, because it does terrible things to naughty children. Then there are the fierce *loupgarous* (loop-gar-oos). These were once humans but their souls have been eaten by demons. The demons then continue to use the bodies for their own purposes. Loupgarous are blamed for everything bad. They cause sickness, a business to fail, or a boyfriend to run away. Even worse are the *vlinbindingues* (vlin-bind-ing-ues). These are nasty loupgarous who wear long, white gowns. They have tall horns and travel in packs, jumping and leaping in the air. You can sell your soul to the vlin-

Haitians practice many religions, including evangelical ministries.

A Mardi Gras parade

bindingues for power, money, or love. But beware when they come to collect their debt! And don't ignore the *zobopes*. They dress in red and fly around at night drinking blood. The *bisago-ouete-peau* also are found hiding in the shadows. They can shed their skin, hiding it in a cool place, and assume a new identity.

One Haitian folktale relates the frightful story of the Bad Uncle (Tonton) and his sack (macoute), who goes around snatching up children. Unfortunately, this story became all too real in Haiti. The Tontons Macoutes were fearsome bullies employed by the Duvaliers. They beat up and assassinated the dictators' enemies.

But belief in these spirits provides answers to Haitians asking why there are problems in their troubled homeland. It is easy to blame the loupgarous, when nobody seems able or willing to help.

Mardi Gras Party

Mardi Gras is a wild blend of all these Christian and ancient African traditions. The festival is traditionally held on the Tuesday before Ash Wednesday. This launches the Christian season of Lent, leading up to Easter. Lent is a season of fasting and penance that lasts for forty days. Subsequently, Mardi Gras provides one last

chance to celebrate before a long, quiet time of reflection. Celebrations, parades, and parties are in every Haitian town. Mardi Gras is a festival of imagination, with pounding music, fancy costumes and floats rolling through the streets. The Mardi Gras carnival is followed by Rara, when every weekend in Lent, bands from the voodoo societies parade around town, asking for donations. The town of Leogane is noted for its Rara marches.

Under the dictators, Mardi Gras and Rara provided a safe chance to protest. This is *diguisement,* or disguising the real meaning of something. For instance, parade units wore the fancy clothes of upper-crust Haitians and strutted down the avenues of Port-au-Prince. There was one difference. They didn't wear any pants. Others dressed as generals and acted totally crazy. Hungry kids portrayed white tourists. They walked around in fancy sunsuits, talked loudly, and stuck out their bellies. Anyone knowing the truth about Haiti's terrible economic and political conditions knew what was going on.

Mardi Gras can be a wild celebration.

A World of Spirits **105**

CHAPTER NINE

Haiti's Recreational Life

Haiti's art is a true expression of the people's heart and soul. The creative celebration of their history and culture takes many forms. Although barely half of the people are literate, storytelling passes the country's heritage from one generation to another. Storytelling parties, or sings, are usually held in some central location on nights when there is a full moon. The moon's light makes it easier to walk along the narrow mountain roads and keeps the demons away.

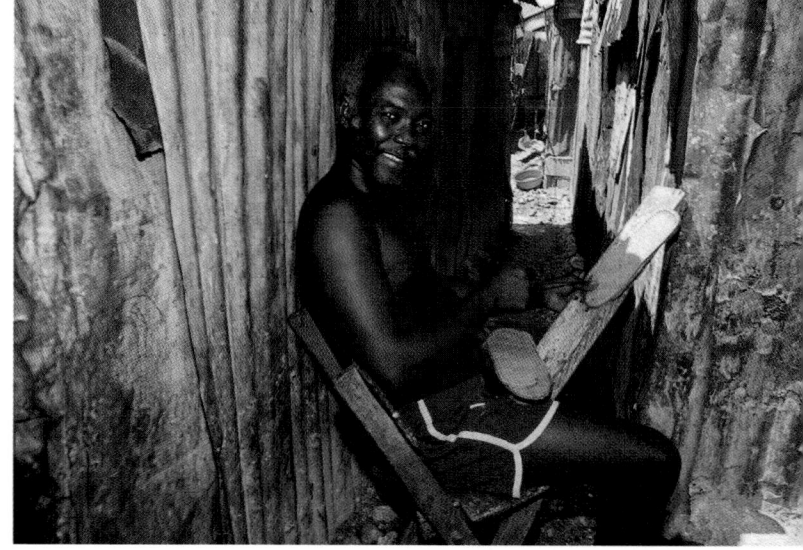

Haitian storytelling often describes everyday life, such as shoemaking.

Whenever there is a sing, friends gather to have a good time. When the time comes to talk, the storyteller says, "Crick!" The listeners gather around, applauding. They say, "Crack!" and the stories start rolling out. In 1901, Haitian writer Georges Sylvain copied down many of these tales in a popular book called *Cric-Crac*.

There are two ways of telling tales in Haiti. In the first, men usually act out the story. Women enter into the fun by singing the songs or chants. The other form is straight storytelling, with all the listeners helping by singing and dancing whenever the time is right. The stories differ from village to village, but the underlying content is the same. Some tales originated in Africa and have taken on a blend of French, Spanish, and Indian tradition. The main themes deal with the family, earning a living, food, money, marriage, and religion. In every tale, there is a moral that helps the listeners learn right from wrong.

Time for Stories

Imagine sitting with some Haitian friends on a warm, moonlit night. The fresh perfume of mangoes and eucalyptus fills the air. It is time for the story called "How the Donkeys Came to Haiti," about how a little boy saved his father from the loas who were disguised as people. When he poked the loas with a stick, they turned

Jacques Roumain

Jacques Roumain (1907–1944) was a poet and novelist who belonged to an upper-class family. He was the grandson of Tancrede Auguste, one of Haiti's presidents. He studied ethnology (a branch of anthropology that concentrates on the culture of people) in Europe. He also conducted research at Columbia University in the United States. He returned to Haiti to found the Office of Ethnology. Roumain was known around the world for his insightful writings on the Haitian way of life (above).

into donkeys. After that story, someone in the circle might tell "The Pig Woman," about how two children named Tito and Lisette got into trouble. They wandered into the forest and were found by an old witch woman. She threatened to eat them. But they were saved by their father in the nick of time. Sometimes the stories are scary, sometimes serious. Yet they are always fun to hear.

Haitian authors usually write in French but a growing number are now writing in Creole. Many great writers have come from this small country. Antoine Dupré is credited with being the first native Haitian poet. It is not known when he was born but he was killed in a duel in 1816. Many of his poems dealt with the meaning of liberty.

Occasionally, Haitian writers have dual professions. One early poet-playwright was also a general. Juste Chanlatte (1766–1828), the count of Rosiers, studied in Paris and returned to his homeland during the reign of King Henri I. He wrote many articles for Haitian newspapers and magazines. Jean-Baptiste Cineas (1895–1958) was a Supreme Court judge who wrote excellent novels in his spare time.

Sometimes, writers have gotten into trouble for their views. "Macanda," a well-known historical poem, was written by Herard Dumesle (1784–1858). Dumesle was president of the national assembly but was exiled to Jamaica when another government came into power. He never saw his country again.

Even today, Haitian writers turn out novels, short stories, plays, and poems. Roger Gaillard, Franck Etienne, Rene Philocete, and Alain Turnier are among the best known contemporary authors. Marie Vieux Chauvet, who was born in 1916, wrote numerous popular novels before she died in 1973 in the United States.

Haitian art is known around the world for its lively themes and dazzling hues. Even the vans or trucks used for mass transportation, called tap-taps, are traveling art works. They are decorated with religious and voodoo symbols. They present a moving dash of color in the streets of the cities.

Haitians also made papier-mâché and copper crafts for decorating their homes and created intricate woodcarvings. In the 1940s, this Haitian primitive art was discovered by tourists. Pieces were brought back to Canada, the United States, and France. The popularity of Haitian art caused a renaissance or

Tap-taps are covered with religious and voodoo symbols.

Some Haitian art is for sale on roadsides.

Le President Florvil Hyppolite by painter Hector Hyppolite

rebirth for the artistic community. More than 5,000 Haitian artists now make their living through many different mediums.

Today, the Milwaukee Art Museum has one of the largest collections of Haitian art outside of Haiti. The collection includes works by Castera Bazile and Hector Hyppolite. Bazile was one of the artists who painted the intricate splash of murals inside the Cathedral of the Holy Trinity in Port-au-Prince. Hyppolite was born in the village of Saint-Marc and painted voodoo scenes. He turned out 253 paintings in three years!

Shutters and doors of Haitian houses are often brightly painted. Homes in the village of Saint-Soleil go one step more. Their interiors explode with color, texture, and form. The town is an artists' community high in the mountains overlooking the capital city. Because many of the painters who live there are voodoo practitioners, their sketches, oils, and watercolors reflect this vibrant aspect of Haitian life.

Painter Issa El Saieh in his gallery

There are several important art galleries in Haiti. In 1944, the Art Center (Centre d'Art) was opened in an old colonial house in Port-au-Prince by an American, DeWitt Clinton Peters. The most important Haitian artists still display their work here. The Museum of Haitian Art is also an excellent place to see the works of well-known Haitian painters and sculptors. There are also numerous private galleries in Port-au-Prince where visitors can buy quality art. George Nader's, Galerie Marassa, Galerie Monnin, and Issa El Saieh are among the best known and most reputable.

The Iron Market

For a less expensive taste of Haitian art, the two-block long Iron Market near the Port-au-Prince harbor has dozens of craftworkers. Straw and wood figurines and brightly colored clothing are among the items for sale. The Iron Market easily earned its name. Many of the buildings are fronted with intricately designed ironwork that has been painted in brilliant colors.

The Haitian art community is not limited only to painting. Sculptor Albert Mangones is known worldwide for his bronzework. One of his most famous works is *Le Maroon Inconnu*, a statue depicting a slave who blew on seashell to start the 1791 slave revolt. The

DeWitt Clinton Peters

DeWitt Clinton Peters taught English in Port-au-Prince in the early 1940s. Bicycling around town, he often passed a boarded-up mansion. Peters thought the site would be a good place for an art school and gallery. One day, he visited Haitian president Elie Lescot and told him of his dream. The president got on the telephone to his secretary and told him to secure the building for Peters. Since the building had been empty and rundown for so long, it took lots of work to clean and repair. But the excited Haitian art community helped.

The first show in the country's new Art Center was held on May 14, 1944. President Lescot even cut the red-and-blue ribbon stretching across the front door. Twenty-three pictures were sold for a total of $500 in U.S. dollars. From this humble beginning, Haitian artists became better recognized and their work increased in value.

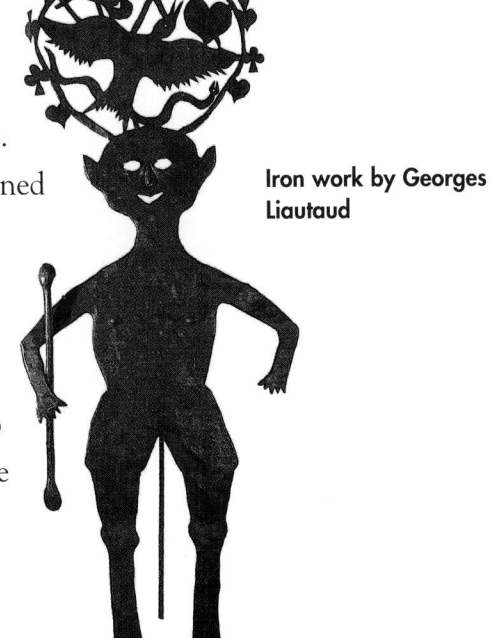

Iron work by Georges Liautaud

The Iron Market in Port-au-Prince

statue sits atop a pedestal in the Champ de Mars, a park near the presidential palace in Port-au-Prince. Georges Liautaud, from Croix-de-Bouquets, was one of Haiti's most famous blacksmiths. He created fabulous works in iron depicting voodoo scenes. His works are displayed in many museums throughout Europe and North America.

Haitian Music Makers

Just about everyone in Haiti makes some sort of music. Kids learn simple tunes on a bamboo flute called the *vaccine*. They also use tambourines, drums, *tchatchas* (marimbas), scrapers, and a trumpet called a *clairon*. Blowing into a seashell also creates an eerie music. For centuries, farmwork has been made easier by singing combites, tunes passed down through the generations of field hands.

Rara is Haiti's special form of music, heard during Lent and on Easter Sunday and Monday. Rara has evolved into another type of Haitian music, the *compas*. This is a pulsing, throbbing rhythm that is influenced by Spanish merengue dances from the neighboring Dominican Republic. Other forms of music are salsa, reggae, soca, and zouk. Singers such Martha-Jean Claude and Toto Bissainthe are known in concert halls and at festivals around the world. Bands like Ram, Sanba-Yo, and Koudjay are popular everywhere they play. Mini Records in Brooklyn, New York, records Haitian tunes for sale in Canada and the United States.

Folk singing is as popular as telling stories. French and African tunes are blended in a fascinating jumble of heritages, especially when performed by Othelo Bayard and his fellow entertainers. The songs often tell intricate stories and are sung at parties called bamboches. These festivities mark birthdays, weddings, and even funerals.

Making music takes many forms.

Dance and Sports

Haitians enjoy dancing. Fast foot movement, swirling skirts, clapping, and leaping are all part of Haitian dance. The Folklore Troupe of Haiti adapted *la danse d'Araignee* (spider

Haitian dance is wild and fast.

A funeral procession in Port-au-Prince

Traditional Ceremonies

Haitians are married and buried in traditional services, usually Roman Catholic since it is the predominant religion.

At a wedding, best clothes are worn and presents given to the bride and groom just like in Canada or the United States. The priest offers mass and presides over the exchange of wedding rings and the marriage vows. Afterwards, a wedding cake is cut and toasts are made. Even poor families offer a wedding meal after the ceremony.

When someone dies, the Catholic rites are generally used. A funeral mass is said, with prayers at the grave-side. A bit of dirt is sprinkled on the casket as it is lowered into the ground. This symbolizes that the body will not last forever. It will decay and soon become part of the earth again.

dance), the *banda*, and the *chairo-pie* from dances done in the rural areas. The company now performs them on international stages. Haitian choreographer Jean Leon Destine also drew on these folk influences for his works.

Sports are important in Haiti but there are no national teams, except for *futbol*, or soccer. Haitian children also play baseball and basketball. They swim in the rivers and the ocean. But their favorite game is soccer. Villages have their own futbol clubs and are proud of local heroes. Kids kick around balls in every open space. Cans or wads of rags are used if no ball is available.

Haitians still talk about the 1974 World Cup soccer championships. For the first time, Haiti qualified to play in the finals held

Teenagers enjoying a soccer game in Cap Haitien

that year in Munich, Germany. These games are the most popular sporting event in the world. The matches are held every four years and watched by millions of television viewers. Regional winners play the world's other best teams. Unfortunately, Haiti lost its three attempts in the first round of play and could not continue on to the next level at the World Cup. But they fought bravely and won the world's admiration.

The World Cup

In the second half of its first match of the World Cup, Haiti's star player Sanon scored first. It was the first time in eleven international matches (1,145 minutes of play) that anyone ever made a goal against Zoff, a tough Italian goalkeeper. The crowd went wild seeing a player from such a small country do so well. Reporters said the game was that of a "dwarf (Haiti) playing a giant (Italy)." Unfortunately for Haiti, Italy eventually won that game, 3–1.

Mountain Training

The high mountains of Haiti make good training grounds for runners, especially on the slopes above Port-au-Prince. Strong legs and lungs are needed for the sharp climbs and descents there. In the 1970s, interest in marathons and long-distance competition running came to Haiti. Several Haitian runners participated in the 1976 Montreal Olympics for the first time. Emmanual St. Hilaire ran the 1,500-meter event. Dieudonne Lamoth participated in the 5,000-meter event. Olmeus Charles ran in the 10,000-meter race. Although none of the three placed in the competitions, the fact that they participated was a great personal accomplishment. All three men had to train themselves. They did not have any outside coaching assistance or sponsorship funding like most other athletes around the world.

Bruny Surin has kept the Haitian running-torch burning. Surin was on the gold-medal team that won the 4x100 relay in the 1996 Olympics in Atlanta, Georgia. He was also a silver medalist in the men's 100-meter run at those summer games. Surin was a twenty-eight-year-old Haitian who moved to Montreal, Canada, when he was six years old. In his team's relay win, they set a Canadian national record at 37.69 seconds. The four men beat out the favored United States team, which came in second.

So from art to sports, despite setbacks and obstacles, the Haitian love of life is readily apparent. That is why the country's creativity and hard work is so widely respected.

Track star Bruny Surin (left), a native of Haiti, now lives in Canada.

Two Sides of Haiti

Noelle lives in a large white house on a side street off the Avenue Pan American in Port-au-Prince. Her father works in Haiti's ministry of education. As an assistant secretary, he works hard to increase the salaries of teachers and to improve their working conditions. Sometimes Noelle accompanies him when he tours schools in the rural areas high in the mountains overlooking Port-au-Prince.

S HE LIKES TO VISIT THE LITTLE TOWN OF PETIONVILLE IN the hills southeast of the capital. She and her father browse through the art galleries and visit artist friends living there. They always stop at a restaurant for a lunch of *pois et riz* (peas and rice) before coming home.

Noelle hopes to become an artist. She especially likes the work of Hilda Williams, who paints colorful scenes with lots of children. Williams was also born in Port-au-Prince and has exhibited in the art center there. That is Noelle's favorite place in all of Port-au-Prince. Noelle would like to be just as good as Williams someday, so she works hard in school. She especially likes the drawing class taught by Sister Angeline.

Noelle attends a private Catholic school not far from her home, so she walks there in just a few minutes. About half the primary schools in Haiti are run by the Roman Catholic Church. Most of her friends attend these private schools.

Some students attend private religious schools.

Others go to rural village schools.

Her final year of primary school is similar to sixth grade in the United States or Canada. Next year, she attends secondary school, which is similar to high school. Both private and public schools in Haiti follow the French model of education. Since French universities accept courses taken in Haitian schools, Noelle may be able to study art in Paris because she is already doing well in every subject. If she doesn't go to France, Noelle will probably attend the State University of Haiti and take social studies. After she graduates, she could travel to the United States or Canada for more schooling. In secondary school, Noelle will take English lessons. Now, she speaks fluent French and a little bit of Creole.

She wants to visit the United States. One of her father's brothers is a sales executive in New Jersey. He represents Haiti's Barbancourt Rum Distillery for an import company in the United States. Rum is a liquor made from sugarcane. Barbancourt flavors its drinks with exotic touches like hibiscus and chocolate. The distillery is more than two hundred years old.

For an hour after school, Noelle has tennis lessons. Her coach is trying out for the Haitian national tennis team, which participated in the 1996 Olympics in Atlanta. Everyone watched the matches on Television National d'Haiti (TNH), the national television of Haiti. After tennis, Noelle studies before supper. She has

Delicious Treats

There are two types of Haitian food. Regular food eaten at home is *cuisine du nord*. This is based in traditional African cooking, with the best food of this kind found around Cap Haitien on the northern coast. A typical dish is tum-tum, a cornmeal mush (left). Fine dining found in restaurants or in a rich person's home is *cuisine bourgeoise*. A meal here might include *escargot* (right), or snails, and other fancy seafood dishes like *lambi*. This is grilled or boiled conch meat found inside sea shells. Another favorite food is *salaise*, which is dried beef served with avocado and plantain.

There are several types of liquor made in Haiti for adults to enjoy. Prestige is a local Haitian beer. *Cremasse* is a holiday drink made of rum and milk. *Selle-bride* is a sweet and spicy rum, while *tafia* is a white rum. There are also plenty of local colas made from tropical fruit.

a big test in her religion class the next morning so she wants to be ready.

Tonight, Anelise, the family cook, is fixing *grillots de porc*. The wonderfully tangy scent of sizzling meat fills the kitchen. This is Noelle's favorite meal. Grillot is grilled pork flavored with oranges

Television is rare. This community has one set they keep outside for everyone to watch.

and served with a spicy sauce called *ti malice*. This sauce is a mixture of lemon, sour oranges, salt, red pepper, and other spices. Noelle agrees that Anelise makes the best hot sauce in the world.

After supper, Noelle's mother and father are going to a reception at Le Plaza Holiday Inn on Rue Capois. A delegation of foreign educators is visiting Haiti. Her dad is hosting a late evening poolside party. Noelle plans on reading a book in her room. She can curl up in her favorite chair, near a window overlooking the garden bursting with orchids.

All the News

There is one government-owned newspaper in Haiti, *Le Moniteur*. It comes out once weekly. Three private daily newspapers are also published in Port-au-Prince. *Le Nouvelliste* is the oldest. It was founded in 1898. *Le Matin* and *Panorama* also provide news. *Libete* is the only Creole-language newspaper. *Le Septentrio* and *L'Union* are two privately owned newspapers in Cap Haitien. All these publications are written in French.

Radio stations use a mix of French and Creole languages. The best news stations are Radio Métropole and Tropic. The Congregational Church operates Radio Lumière. Stations can pick up Radio France, the British Broadcast Company, and Voice of America. Télé Haiti, a commercial television station, often broadcasts programs from France, Canada, the United States, and Latin America.

Before going to bed, she listens to Radio Nouveau Monde before having a snack of *pain patate*, a pudding made of grated potato, figs, banana, and sugar, prepared by Anelise. Radio Nouveau Monde is her favorite because it plays the latest rock music. Noelle thinks that some of the other stations, such the government-owned Radio Nationale, have too many talk shows.

Jean lives on a farm near Hinche, a regional capital. This a six-hour bus ride northeast of Port-au-Prince. The closest village is Ville-Bonheur, reached by a dirt road off Route National 3, the main road. A church here was built more than one hundred years ago on the site where some local people reported seeing the Virgin Mary sitting in a tree. Jean wants to believe that is true but he isn't sure. So when he goes to mass on Sunday, he keeps looking around. Maybe he will see a saint sometime.

The sacred Saut d'Eau waterfall

Practitioners of voodoo, including some of Jean's relatives, come to his village every July. They hike back into the hills to the misty Saut d'Eau waterfall where they bathe in the sacred water. The visitors perch on the moss-covered rock ledges around the pools at the base of the rushing falls before jumping into the water. Jean has watched their voodoo services many times. When the hungry outsiders leave, they buy tomatoes and onions grown on the small family plot. Jean and his brothers and sisters sell the vegeta-

Vendors selling beans and other foods in Port-au-Prince

bles along the side of the dusty road that leads to the waterfall. The children are very polite. They say "*bon jour*" (good morning) to everyone they meet in the morning and "*bon soir*" (good evening) later in the day.

Although his home is far from Port-au-Prince, Jean has visited the Haitian capital several times. His aunt is Anelise, Noelle's cook. He likes visiting there because Anelise always feeds him well. Jean has never met Noelle, but he has seen her coming home from school. Anelise's son, cousin Paul, drives a taxi in Port-au-Prince and gives Jean a ride whenever he comes to visit him there.

The last time he came to the capital, Jean was really scared. Paul went very fast, roaring down the Rue Pavée past the Episcopal cathedral and honking his horn at the other taxis. Some patrolling soldiers from the multinational force who helped President Aristide return to power waved at them. Paul said they were blancs, white men from the United States, and were usually okay. Off-duty soldiers tip him well whenever Paul acts as a guide during their day off. "All blancs have lots of money," says Paul.

Jean helps his father work the family farm and is charge of the family goat. He also keeps an eye on his younger brothers so they don't get into trouble. Jean seldom has time for school because his family needs him to work at home. He is glad that he can write his name, even though he has a hard time reading. Nobody else in his family can read, so they are proud of Jean.

This evening, he hopes to have some delicious fried green plantains, a fruit similar to bananas. During the day, all Jean has to eat is a small dish of *petit mil*, a grain similar to millet. He is very hungry because he worked hard pulling weeds in the garden. Jean started working at 6 A.M. and finally finished his chores late in the evening.

Even though his house is small and crowded, it is good to come home. The walls are of plastered mud, but it has a tin roof, which keeps out the rain. Some of their neighbors have only leaking, moldy straw roofs. Until supper, Jean sits in front of his house and talks about futbol with his four younger brothers. Jean sleeps in the same bed with them. Toureau, Rene, Nicolas, and Louis are fine when they are awake. But too many feet and arms are tossed about when they are sleeping. There is a lot of punching and kicking before sleeping. They share two

Many children have chores on their farms.

National Holidays

Independence Day	January 1
Heroes of the Independence Day	January 2
Shrove Monday	Varies
Shrove Tuesday	Varies
Good Friday	Varies
Easter	Varies
Pan-American Day	April 14
Labor Day	May 1
Flag Day	May 18
National Sovereignty Day	May 22
Assumption	August 15
United Nations Day	October 24
All Souls' Day	November 2
Army Day and Commemoration of the Battle of Vertieres	Varies
Discovery Day	December 5
Christmas Day	December 25

Looking out over Port-au-Prince

thin blankets and often fight over who gets the largest share.

A House Too Small

The boys' two older sisters, Michele and Gisou, sleep across the tiny bedroom. They complain about noise from the brothers, but there is nothing their mother or father can do. The house is simply too small. The family would have been even larger but four older brothers became sick and died before Jean was born. He knows his mother and father miss them.

Jean dreams of moving to Port-au-Prince someday. He might drive a taxi like Paul or get a job in a hotel. That would bring in some good money, enough to send home. But he has a long way to go until then. Just like Jean, Haiti is looking forward to a more promising future.

Timeline

Haitian History

Columbus visits Haiti.	1492
Haiti becomes an official French colony.	1697
Haitian Revolution launched by mulatto and black rebels.	1789
France loses Dominican Republic to Haiti.	1801
French withdraw from Hispaniola	1804
Emperor Jean-Jacques Dessalines is assassinated and a civil war follows.	1806
Haiti loses the Dominican Republic.	1808–1809
Haiti reconquers Santo Domingo.	1822
Santo Domingo becomes separate nation called the Dominican Republic.	1844
Twenty different presidents rule Haiti.	1867–1915
U.S. forces land in Haiti in response to growing violence.	1915
U.S. troops withdraw.	1934
Crises occur with the Dominican Republic over abuse of Haitian refugees.	1937–1938
Dusmarsais Estimé becomes president.	1946
Communist party is outlawed.	1948
Estimé is deposed.	1950
François Duvalier is elected president and assumes dictatorial powers.	1957

World History

1492	Columbus arrives in North America.
1500s	The Reformation leads to the birth of Protestantism.
1776	The Declaration of Independence is signed.
1789	The French Revolution begins.
1865	The American Civil War ends.
1914	World War I breaks out.
1917	The Bolshevik Revolution brings Communism to Russia.
1929	Worldwide economic depression begins.
1939	World War II begins, following the German invasion of Poland.
1957	The Vietnam War starts.

Haitian History		World History
Duvalier proclaims presidency for life.	1964	
Jean-Claude (Baby Doc) Duvalier gains control after the death of his father.	1971	
Baby Doc flees to France.	1985–1986	
	1989	The Berlin Wall is torn down, as Communism crumbles in Eastern Europe.
Fr. Jean-Bertrand Aristide is elected president.	1990	
Military forces oust Aristide; refugees flee to the United States.	1991	
The United Nations imposes a worldwide oil, arms, and financial embargo on Haiti.	1993	
Aristide returns as Haiti's President.	1994	
U.N. peacekeeping force takes over responsibility of Haiti	1995	
Rene Préval is sworn in as president with a small U.N. peacekeeping force on hand.	1996	1996 — Bill Clinton is reelected U.S. president.

Fast Facts

Official name: Republic of Haiti

The countryside near Jacmel

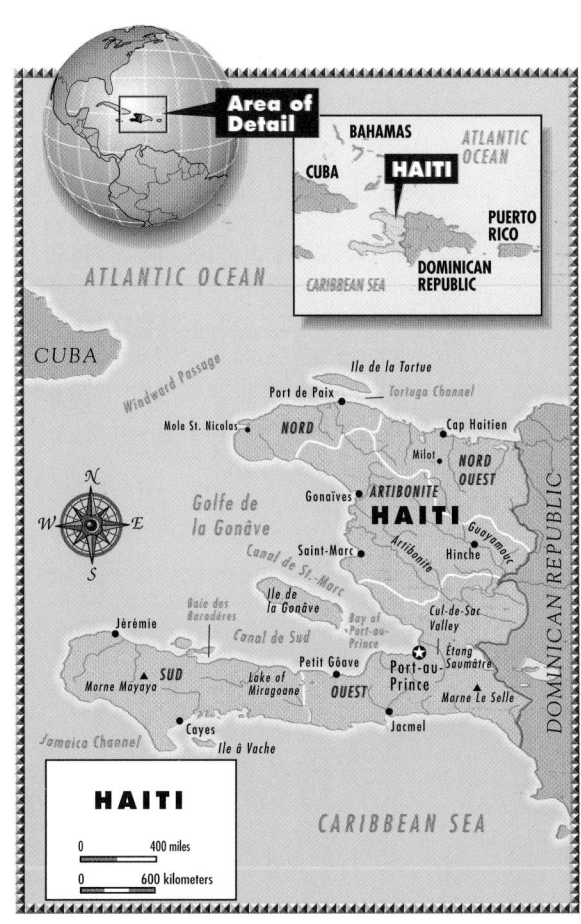

Capital: Port-au-Prince

Official languages: French and Creole

Flag of Haiti

Father Jean-Bertrand Aristide

Official religion:	none
National anthem:	"*La Dessalinienne*" or in English "Song of Dessalines" written by Justin L'herisson and music by Nicholas Geffrard
Government:	Multiparty republic with two legislative houses (Senate and Chamber of Deputies)
Area:	10,695 square miles (27,700 sq km) excluding off-shore islands
Bordering countries:	Haiti is bordered on the east by the Dominican Republic and to the west (separated by a thin body of water) by Cuba.
Highest elevation:	Morne la Selle 8,793 feet (2,680 m)
Lowest elevation:	Sea level along coast
Average temperatures:	70°F (20°C) in the mountains to 87°F (31°C) along the coast

Average annual rainfall:

Cayes	79 inches (201 cm)
Cap Haitien	59 inches (151 cm)
Hinche	57 inches (144 cm)
Fort Liberté	52 inches (130 cm)
Jacmel	52 inches (133 cm)
Port-de-Paix	46 inches (118 cm)
Gonaïves	20 inches (52 cm)

National population: (1995 est.) 7,180,000

Population (1994 est.) of largest cities in Haiti:

Port-au-Prince	743,000
Cap Haitien	68,000
Cayes	36,000
Gonaïves	34,000

Famous landmarks: There are many castles on the shores of Haiti. A few, such as Fort Dauphin near Cayes, were built in 1732 by the French to keep out enemies. Many others, however, were built by the Haitians themselves, like the Fortress des Platons in Cayes and the Citadelle in Cap Haitien. The Haitians are also a very religious people with many beautiful cathedrals around the island. Many date back to French occupation, such as the ones in Port-au-Prince and Gonaïves.

In Petit Goave, a tiny little town 57 miles (92 km) north of Port-au-Prince, the once regal home of Emperor Faustin I, the Relais de l'Empereur, can be found. Also near Cap Haitien lies the ruins of King Henri Christophe's royal palace, Sans Souci. It used to house a printing shop, a garment factory, a distillery, and an army barracks, among many other things.

Industry: Agriculture makes up about 41.3 percent of Haiti's gross domestic product (GDP). Important crops include coffee, sugar, bananas, corn, and rice. Tourism and banking contribute about 33.9 percent to the GDP. Manufacturing of food products adds 11.1 percent to the GDP. Major industries in Haiti are sugar refining and textile manufacture. Mining accounts for a very small portion of Haiti's GDP: 0.1 percent. Marble, limestone, and copper are extracted in small quantities.

Currency: Haiti's currency is called the gourde.
One gourde equals 100 centimes.
1997 exchange rate U.S.$1 = 16.18 gourdes.

A government building in Port-au-Prince

Weights and measures:	Haiti uses both the metric system and English measure.
Literacy:	53%

Common words and phrases:

Bonjour	Hello
Ki jan ou rélé?	What is your name?
Kouman ou yé?	How are you?
Gras a Dieu,	Thanks God, I'm fine.
m pa pi mal	(Haitians attribute all things of life to the Diety, so God must be thanked for all things good.)
Papa!	Man (as in "Man, that's crazy!")
Sa rélé senp	That's called magic
M rélé . . .	My name is . . .
Oui, maché	Yes, my dear
Ou a tiré	You'll get your money
lajan ou	out of it
Pinga reken-you	Watch out for the sharks.
Mouen fét . . .	I was born in . .

To Find Out More

Nonfiction

▶ Anthony, Suzanne. *Haiti*. New York: Chelsea House, 1989.

▶ Goldish, Meish. *Crisis in Haiti*. Brookfield, CT: Millbrook Press, 1995.

▶ Tekavec, Valerie. *Haitian Teenagers Speak Out*. New York: Rosen Publishing Group, 1995.

▶ Weddle, Ken. *Haiti in Pictures*. Minneapolis, MN: Lerner Publications, 1989.

Biographies

▶ Aristide, Jean-Bertrand. *Aristide: An Autobiography*. Maryknoll, NY: Orbis Books, 1993.

▶ Hurston, Zora Neale, and Ishmael Reed. *Tell My Horse: Voodoo and Life in Haiti and Jamaica*. New York: HarperCollins, 1990.

Fiction

▶ Danticat, Edwidge. *Krik? Krak? Stories.* New York: Soho Press, 1995

▶ Lieberman, Laurence. *The Creole Mephistopheles.* New York: Scribners, 1988.

▶ Temple, Frances. *Taste of Salt: A Story of Modern Haiti.* New York: Orchard Books, 1992.

▶ Temple, Frances. *Tonight by the Sea: A Novel.* New York: Orchard Books, 1997.

▶ Wolkstein, Diane. *The Banza, A Haitian Story.* New York: Dial Press, 1981.

Folklore

▶ Bontemps, Arna, and E. Simms Campbell. Illustrated by Langston Hughes. *Popo and Fifina.* New York: Oxford University Press Children's Books, 1993

▶ Des Pres, François Turenne. *Children of Yayoute: Folk Tales of Haiti.* New York: Universe Press, 1994.

▶ Dobrin, Arnold. *Josephine's 'Magination: A Tale of Haiti.* New York: Scholastic, 1992.

▶ Reasoner, Charles E. *Night Owl and the Rooster: A Haitian Legend.* NJ: Troll Associates, 1995.

▶ Wolkstein, Diane. Illustrated by Elss Henriquez. *The Magic Orange Tree: And Other Haitian Folktales.* New York: Schocken Books, 1997.

Videotapes

▶ *Haiti: Waters of Sorrow.* Directed by Jean-Paul Cornu. The Cousteau Society/Turner Home Entertainment, 1991.

Websites

▶ **Haiti: A Country Study**
http://lcweb2.loc.gov/frd/cs/httoc.html
The Country Studies/Area
Handbook Program of the Library of
Congress provides an in-depth study
of the geography, history, and culture
of Haiti.

▶ **CIA World Fact Book on Haiti**
http://www.odci.gov/cia/publications/
nsolo/factbook/ha.htm
A full range of facts and figures
about Haiti maintained by the
Central Intelligence Agency.

▶ **The Art of Haiti**
http://www.medalia.net/
A virtual art gallery of the work of
Haiti's best artists.

Organizations and Embassies

▶ **Haitian Embassy**
2311 Massachusetts Avenue, NW
Washington, DC 20008
(202) 332-4090

▶ **Haitian Consulate in New York**
271 Madison Avenue,
17th Floor
New York, NY 10016
(212) 697-9767

Index

black magic and, 101
ceremonial flags, 98–99
Christianity compared to,
    95, 97, 100
doctors, 98
François Duvalier and, 100
hounfors, 98
houngan (priest), 97

mambo (priestess), 97
Saut d'Eau waterfall, *123*
symbolism in, 100

W–X–Y–Z
waterfalls, 27, *27*
waterways, *23*
White House, 60

White-winged warbler, 30
Williams, Hilda, 119
Windward Passage, 16
work songs, 90
World Cup soccer competition, 115–
    116

zobopes, 104

Meet the Author

ESEARCHING THE HISTORY AND CULTURE OF A COUNTRY IS AN important part of writing a book about it. Martin Hintz used numerous library resources as well as the Internet to discover fascinating facts about Haiti. He also spoke with Haitians, whose conversation tells the real tale of their homeland. In addition, Hintz went to art galleries to look at Haitian art, read stories by Haitian writers, and he checked with government and private relief

agency sources. He even tried Haitian food. Hintz also interviewed Haitian president Rene Préval at a summit of Caribbean leaders in Barbados in 1997.

From all this study, it was obvious that the Haitian people have many wonderful attributes. They are courageous in the face of danger. They are optimistic when challenges loom. They have fascinating traditions. They want you to learn more about them.

Photo Credits